D1047095

Illustrated by Al Fiorentino

Meriwether Lewis

Boy Explorer

Meriwether Lewis

Boy Explorer

By Charlotta M. Bebenroth

Aladdin Paperbacks

First Aladdin Paperbacks edition August 1997
Copyright © 1946, 1953, 1962, by Charlotta M. Bebenroth

Aladdin Paperbacks
An imprint of Simon & Schuster
Children's Publishing Division
1230 Avenue of the Americas
New York, NY 10020

Printed and bound in the United States of America

10   9   8   7   6   5   4

Library of Congress Cataloging-in-Publication Data

Bebenroth, Charlotta M., 1890–
Meriwether Lewis, boy explorer / by Charlotta M. Bebenroth ; illustrated by
Al Fiorentino. — 1st Aladdin Paperbacks ed.
      p.   cm.
Summary: Relates events from the childhood and youth of the boy who grew
up to become an explorer of the American West.
ISBN 0-689-81740-1
1. Lewis, Meriwether, 1774–1809—Childhood and youth—Juvenile
literature.   2. Explorers—West (U.S.)—Biography—Juvenile literature.
3. Lewis and Clark Expedition (1804–1806)—Juvenile literature.
4. West (U.S.)—Discovery and exploration—Juvenile literature.
[1. Lewis, Meriwether, 1774–1809—Childhood and youth.   2. Explorers.]
I. Fiorentino, Al, ill.   II. Title.
            F592.7B43   1997
   917.804'2—dc21   [B]   97-9990   CIP   AC

To Hattie in friendship

Illustrations

Full pages

Numerous smaller illustrations

Contents

Meriwether Lewis

Boy Explorer

Locust Hill

IT WAS A warm August morning in Albemarle County in western Virginia over two hundred years ago.

A blue haze lay over the foothills of the Blue Ridge Mountains. The rising sun twinkled on the green leaves as they danced in the morning breeze. Far away in the forest, a lonesome crow cawed loudly.

A tiny chipmunk chattered in angry surprise as two figures slipped quietly out of the forest and stood beside him. He ran to safety under the roots of a giant oak tree. There he looked with curious eyes at the newcomers.

11

One was a tall, strong boy about eight years old, who stopped for a moment to look down into the valley. A large black dog followed at his heels.

A rifle in the boy's hand, his deerskin hunting suit and the opossum which he laid on the ground showed that he had been hunting. In fact, young Meriwether Lewis had been out all night, alone in the forest.

The black dog sat close to his master and barked softly as he pointed his nose toward the valley. Meriwether patted him gently.

"Hungry, are you? All right then. We'll go home to breakfast. Come along."

They started down the mountainside toward a large plantation which lay below. The Big House of the plantation could be seen among the locust trees. The trees had given it the name of "Locust Hill." It was the family home. In it lived busy Mrs. Lewis and her three children.

Jane was the oldest. She was twelve. Meriwether came next, then Reuben, who was the youngest. The wide acres of fields, pastures, forests, the servants' quarters and the Big House all belonged to Meriwether. Sometimes the fact worried him. When the servants came to him with their troubles he wished that he knew more and could give better advice.

His father had been an officer in General Washington's army and had died four years before. He had been home on leave and had caught a slight cold. Traveling through bad weather back to the camp, he became much worse from chill and fatigue. He stopped at "The Farm," the plantation home of Uncle Nicholas Lewis and there he died.

Meriwether's mother and Uncle Nicholas Lewis had charge until he grew older, but the servants called him Mister Merne and looked to him to do things for them.

Smoke began to rise from the chimneys of the servants' quarters. A white plume of smoke puffed up from the kitchen chimney of the Big House. Faster and faster came the smoke. Then came a shower of sparks. Someone was in a hurry to get breakfast started.

Thinking of the good meal to come, Meriwether began to feel hungry and hurried his footsteps. Another shower of sparks came out of the chimney. Chloe, the family cook, must have slept late and was burning pine kindling, to make such a high, quick fire. His mother would be angry if she saw it. Sparks often started deadly fires.

As Meriwether drew near the house, he saw a thin curl of smoke coming, not from the chimney, but from the roof of the Big House itself! A spark must have fallen on a dry shingle where it began to blaze.

He threw aside the opossum and his gun and

began to run, calling at the top of his voice, "Fire! Fire! Bring a ladder! Hurry!"

Doors flew open as if by magic. Mrs. Lewis, his sister Jane, and little five-year-old Reuben ran out, followed by the house servants. They looked up at the roof. Servants from the quarters came too. In the excitement they forgot to bring a ladder. Meanwhile the curl of smoke grew larger and larger. It would not do to wait any longer.

Two of the servants, Cuffy and Job, ran back for a ladder. Meriwether quickly climbed a large locust tree that grew near the house. Up, up he went, and then far out on a branch that hung over the roof. He leaped from the branch to the roof. Then he crawled carefully up to where the fire had begun to blaze.

Chloe wrung her hands as she watched, and cried to Mrs. Lewis, "Miss Lucy, that boy's going to fall off the roof and break his neck!"

"I know, Chloe! But what else can we do? It would be worse if the roof burned over our heads?" Then she spoke firmly to the men. "Cuffy and Job, get that ladder against the house. Now, Cuffy, up with this pail of water, and see whether you can help put out that fire!"

Up on the roof Meriwether was working fast. He tried to beat out the flame with his cap. Sparks still glowed brightly underneath. He tore off a blazing shingle. It burned his hands, and he tossed it down into the yard. He was glad when Cuffy reached his side with a pail of water.

Together they poured the water carefully on the roof. Job brought another pailful and this put out the very last spark. They waited awhile to see if all was safe and then went down the ladder.

Uncle Frank Meriwether had just arrived to spend the day. He said in a hearty voice, "Very good, my boy! Very good, indeed! Now let me see your hands. Ahem! Just as I thought. You burned them when you pulled up that shingle. Chloe, we need your help. Bring oil and bandages so Miss Lucy can take care of these hands. Then what about something to eat? We're all mighty hungry!"

Meriwether's hands were oiled and bandaged. Then the family sat down to a hearty meal of baked ham, corn bread, mush, and milk. Uncle Frank said he would go up on the roof with Job after breakfast. He would see that the roof was made as good as new.

Meriwether ate quietly but was glad to tell of the night birds and animals he had seen during his night in the forest.

Later in the morning Uncle Frank asked, "Where's Meriwether?"

"Gone to bed for a nap," answered Mrs. Lewis. "He was out in the woods all night, you know."

"That child! Who was with him?"

"No one. He likes to go alone. Sometimes he hunts, but I think he's more interested in the night life of the forest than in hunting."

"He's too young to go off alone like that!"

"That's true, but since his father died, he's had to take a man's place on the plantation, as you saw today. But for him the house might be in ashes by now."

"Yes, it took quick thinking to put out that fire. You can be proud of the boy. He is smart for his age and well liked."

"Yes," agreed Mrs. Lewis with a sigh, "that's all true, but sometimes I feel sorry that he has never had time to be just a little boy."

Michie Tavern

MERIWETHER rode with his Uncle Nicholas along a red dirt road through the forest. There were signs of a coming storm and the horses were restless. Birds flew hither and yon looking for shelter.

Heavy thunder rolled across the sky. The earth trembled beneath the horses' hoofs. Sharp lightning zigzagged down a dark cloud. A cold wind stirred the forest trees. Large drops of rain pattered on the leaves.

"Well, Merne," said Nicholas Lewis, using the family nickname for the boy, "I think it's time to look for shelter. Michie Tavern is not far away and we can hurry the horses. Come along, my boy!"

Away they went! Meriwether's small bay mare galloped almost at the heels of his Uncle's big black horse. Loose clods of earth flew from under the horses' hoofs. Frightened birds fluttered in the bushes as they passed.

Then, just as the rain came down in a blinding sheet, the two riders raced into the innyard. An old black man stood under the roof of an open shed. He was waiting to take their horses.

"Saw you coming, Mister Lewis," he chuckled. "Those horses did sure enough go! Just step along inside. Governor Thomas Jefferson came in just before you."

This was good news. Mr. Jefferson was a close friend of the Lewis family. He lived only a few miles away. His home was on a beautiful mountaintop.

People liked Mr. Jefferson. He was a kind

man. He was wise too. Because of his great ability he had been elected Governor of the State of Virginia.

Now his term of office was over. He was glad to be at home again.

Meriwether had never seen the inside of an inn. His heart beat a little faster as he went toward the big front door. He had made very few trips with his parents. At such times they had stayed overnight at the plantation homes of kinsfolk and friends along the way, so going into a tavern was something new.

The main room of the tavern was long and low. A log fire blazed in the large fireplace at the far end of the room. Mr. Jefferson sat before it, talking with some strange men.

Thomas Jefferson was a tall, thin man with red hair. When he spoke everyone listened.

The innkeeper hurried forward to welcome Uncle Nicholas. In no time at all Meriwether found himself, the only boy in the room, seated among a group of men.

They were talking about Indians, and the boy leaned forward with shining eyes. It was not every day that one could hear talk of these people from the far country on the other side of the mountains.

A short gray-haired man was speaking. Mr. Jefferson had called him Trader Jones. "Yes, I traded with the Indians. I've been going out there for years. The goods are carried on pack horses. My wise old gray mare wears a bell and leads the pack train. I never know what'll happen before I get back to the settlements."

Trader Jones warmed his large red hands before the leaping flames.

"Now take my first trip into Kentucky," he went on. "I was only fourteen. I went with my two big brothers for the winter hunting. We made camp in a valley. The hunting was good.

One day I went off by myself tracking a deer. The deer ran into a thick forest and I followed. Three Indians sprang from behind trees and took me prisoner.

"They were Shawnees traveling north to their home village. They dragged me with them day after day until every bone in my body ached."

When Trader Jones paused, with a faraway look in his eyes, Meriwether asked anxiously, "Did you get away soon?"

"There was no chance. Once at night I tried to creep into the darkness. The brave on watch was dozing, but he heard me. They tied my hands and feet after that."

"What did the Indians do?" asked Meriwether curiously.

"The sentry beat me with a stick, but the next morning he gave me a handful of parched corn. It was all that he or the others had to eat.

"The trail was long and hard, but I had to

keep going. One day when we were crossing a river, the thin ice broke. An Indian was near me and we both fell in. The others helped us out but our clothes were wet. We didn't stop— just kept going.

"At evening we came to the Shawnee village. Everyone turned out to meet us. I never heard such yells. The beating of tom-toms was enough to make one deaf. All the Indian boys were glad to see a captive. They pointed at me. They jumped up and down and shouted. I was glad to be pushed at last into a wigwam. An old woman with a fierce dog was to guard me. Every time I moved, the dog growled, so I lay still."

"What were they going to do with you?" asked Meriwether.

"That's what I wanted to know.

"I didn't sleep much that night for wondering what the morning would bring. When morning came, I knew!

26

"All the boys and young men gathered outside my wigwam. They stood in two rows facing each other. Each warrior held a heavy stick. One of them led me to the head of the line. I knew that he expected me to run the gauntlet—and I was afraid."

Meriwether opened his mouth to ask what a gauntlet was. Just in time he remembered the look his uncle had given him when he asked his last question—and he closed his lips without speaking. Mr. Jefferson, who saw everything, laughed and said, "Trader Jones, why not tell our young friend what a gauntlet is?"

"A gauntlet is just what I've told you about. It's made up of two lines of Indians. Each one is armed with a club. The prisoner runs between the lines. As he runs the Indians beat him with their sticks. That's to see if he's brave. Usually the runner is badly hurt before he gets to the end of the line.

"Well, there I stood. My feet wouldn't move. One of the men gave me a push. At the same moment a big fellow in the line reached over and gave me a nasty cut on the leg. Blood began to run. The pain was bad, so bad that I forgot to be afraid. Before the one who had hit me knew what I was up to, I twisted the club from his hand and swung at him. Down he went!

"Others came running, but I backed up to a tree and let them feel the weight of the club. Soon there were three more on the ground. The rest drew back and rushed me from all sides. There were so many that in no time at all they would have had me down, but the Indian boys had a big surprise. A whistle and a sharp order from the chief, Big Bear, stopped the fight.

"He motioned for me to follow him to his wigwam. There his mother rubbed my cuts with bear fat. They needed more braves in the village. He thought I would do. The next week

I was taken into the tribe. Even then an Indian was always near to see that I didn't steal away.

"Spring came at last and the Shawnees were ready to travel north to the Great Lakes. One evening the chief placed my gun and powder horn beside me. He said that I could either go north with the tribe or return to my people.

"Well, I hurried back toward Kentucky. It took some time for me to find my brothers. All their things were packed and they were ready to return home. They had had enough of the wilderness and were glad to be going back to the settlement. For me the wild country beyond the mountains is still a wonderful place, wide and free. I'll be trading there for some time to come."

"Did you ever see Big Bear again? Was he angry because you went away?" exclaimed Meriwether. All the men smiled because they had wanted to ask the same question.

"Big Bear is my friend. He's an old man now, but still glad to see me in his village. He expected me to return to my own people."

"What's on the other side of the mountains?" asked Meriwether eagerly.

"Long rivers and beautiful valleys and, far, far to the west, mountains higher than our own Blue Ridge Mountains. That is what the Indians tell us. It's a big land waiting for someone to travel up and down and then come back to tell us what is there."

"Are you going exploring, Meriwether?" asked Uncle Nicholas with a smile.

"Someday I hope to go where no white man has ever been," the boy replied.

"To explore the western lands as far as the Pacific Ocean is a job that needs doing," said Mr. Jefferson. "Meriwether will have to wait until he's older, though. It is a man's work."

A ray of sunshine stole into the room as the

last bit of thunder rumbled in the distance. The storm was over. The guests arose.

"Come, Merne. We must be on our way," said Nicholas Lewis. "Gentlemen, it was a pleasure to meet you here."

As the bay mare and the big black horse trotted homeward, Meriwether made up a little song which he hummed in time to the horses' hoofbeats. The words went like this:

"Someday I'm going west!
Someday I'm going west!
Someday I'm going
'way out west!"

31

Exploring the Cavern

PEACHY GILMER and David Wood had come with their mothers to visit the Lewises for a month or two. This was a short visit. Sometimes visitors came and stayed for many months. They brought their children and servants too.

Peachy and David were cousins and a few years older than Meriwether. He was a better hunter, though, and knew his way about in field and forest better than they. The boys were full of pranks and jokes which they tried out on everyone in the Big House.

One morning Aunt Mary Gilmer spoke of going home in a day or two. Peachy Gilmer decided then that it was time the boys made their trip into the mountains. They had talked about it often.

The three boys with Ruff, the black dog, set out that same morning. They had plenty of lunch with them and planned to be gone all day.

As they rode along David Wood had a bright idea. "Let's go and explore a cave instead of climbing up the mountains," he said.

"That's a good idea. Let's," agreed Peachy. "Where's the cave? How big is it?"

"There are ever so many caves in the mountains," said Meriwether. "I've never been in any except the little ones, though. Some go far, far back into the hills."

"Let's explore a big one. Maybe we'll find an Indian treasure," said David.

"Perhaps we ought to wait until Uncle Frank or Uncle Nicholas could go with us," suggested Meriwether slowly. "Mother made me promise that I would never go into a big cave unless an older person is along."

"Well, you won't be alone. We'll be right with you. We are older, too," said David.

"Come on! Let's find a big one."

They rode across the fields until they came to the mountain lands. Here they tied the horses and crawled in among some bushes that hid an opening between two large rocks.

"There's a cave in there," said Meriwether. "I know because it echoes. Try it."

The boys took turns calling into the opening. Sure enough, an answering echo came back each time. The boys listened with delight.

"I'm going in!" exclaimed Peachy. "It sounds like a big one and I want to see a real cave."

"How are you going to see it?" asked David. "It'll be dark as night in there."

"Well, we'll take some torches. Merne, what's the best wood for torches? You tell us."

34

"Pine knots are good. They burn a long time and throw a bright light," said Meriwether.

It took some time to find just the wood the boys wanted. At last they cut several branches from a large pine tree blown down in a storm.

Merne gathered some dry leaves. Then he took out the flint and steel which he always carried in his pocket. He struck the flint and steel together. This made sparks. The sparks fell among the dry leaves and kindled a little fire. He lighted a twig and, when the tip blazed up, lighted a branch of the pine tree. This torch he handed to Peachy, who had crawled between the rocks into the cave.

"Whee-e-e!" called Peachy shrilly. "What a big place! You ought to see it. Bring the sticks and come on in!"

That was enough for the two boys outside. Without another word they dropped on hands and knees and crept into the cave.

The light from Peachy's torch showed the cave to be both long and high. They could see only a small part of it. The far corners were in darkness, but what they saw was beautiful.

The boys looked and looked while the light flickered on what seemed to be long icicles of dazzling white. They hung from the ceiling or pointed up from the floor.

"They're made by limewater dripping," said David. "I read about them in a book. Pretty, don't you think?"

The others were speechless with surprise.

"Listen!" said David. "I hear water running over there."

The sound led the boys farther into the cave until at last they stopped on the bank of a rushing stream.

David said, "I'll jump across. It's nothing."

Peachy seized him by the arm and held tight. "Wait! You might slip," he said. "Let's try with a stick!"

He thrust first a short stick and then a longer one into the stream, but they did not touch the bottom. "Too deep. Let's go back."

"No," answered David. "Go back if you want to. I'm going to see what's over there."

As he spoke he jumped and landed safely on the other side.

Peachy followed and Meriwether was left alone. He wondered if his legs were long enough for such a jump.

"Come on!" called David sharply. "The torch is going out."

The other bank did not rise as high above the water as the one on which Meriwether stood. He went back a few feet and made a running jump. The jump carried him across the stream, but as he came down on the opposite side his feet slipped on the wet stones. He went straight into the water.

Peachy shouted, "Hold on, Merne! Hold on!" There was nothing for Meriwether to hold onto, though.

David carried the blazing torch and ran along the bank calling, "Swim, Merne! Swim!" Then he cried, "Help! Help!"

The shouts echoed back from all sides of the cave. Ruff added to the noise with one sharp bark. Then he sprang into the water to swim beside his young master.

David called, "Quick, Peachy! Give me another torch!"

Peachy answered in a queer voice, "We left the sticks on the other side." Just then David's torch went out and left the cave in blackness.

Peachy and David called again and again, at the top of their voices, "Help! Help!" Down in the stream Meriwether clung to Ruff's neck with one hand. With the other he reached out for a narrow ledge of rock on the other bank near which the water had carried him. He seized it and managed to pull Ruff up beside him. Behind the ledge the rocky bank rose steeply. Meriwether called to the other boys to tell them where he was.

Peachy and David groped their way to a point just opposite him. They kept yelling for help and urged Meriwether to hold on.

After what seemed hours, but was really only a few minutes, Peachy saw a light. The light came nearer. It was carried by a boy who was running along the bank above the little ledge where Meriwether and Ruff were standing.

"What's the matter here?" the boy called.

"Our cousin fell in the water, and our torch went out," gasped Peachy. "He's down there on your side."

The boy placed his torch against a stone and took a coil of wild grapevine from over his arm. Meriwether could see now that the bank rose about five feet above him.

The boy threw one end to Meriwether and said "Hold tight! I'll pull while you climb!"

"Ruff—I can't leave him!" gasped Meriwether. His teeth chattered when he spoke. He was chilled from being in the icy water.

"We'll get the dog too. Tie this other vine around him. Then come!"

Meriwether went up slowly, placing his feet in holes in the rock. Near the top the big boy caught him by the shoulder and helped him over the edge.

Then came Ruff's turn. He could not climb, so the boys pulled him up slowly while Meriwether called and coaxed.

At the top Ruff shook himself so that water flew all around, and then he rushed over to lick his master's hands.

Peachy and David went back to where they had crossed the stream. By the torchlight it took only a moment. They jumped to the other side again, and joined Meriwether and his rescuer.

"Let's get out of here. I've had enough of caves." David shivered. Then he asked the strange boy, "How did you happen to come in? You don't know how glad we were to see you. What's your name?"

"My name is Will Clark. I saw the horses

outside and heard someone cry for help. There have been accidents like this before. Many people have been lost in caves. So I cut a couple of vines, lighted a torch, and came in. Let's get out of here. We'd better make a fire and dry this young fellow's clothes."

They walked along the bank which sloped gradually downward. Soon they saw the light at the entrance to the cave.

The boys soon had a big fire blazing. Meriwether sat beside it and toasted himself. It was good to get the chill out of his bones. The others dried his clothes on sticks held over the fire while he wore Peachy's coat.

Peachy asked Will Clark if he knew George Rogers Clark, who had once lived in the neighborhood.

Will answered, "George Rogers Clark, who won the Northwest Territory, is my brother. I hope I can do something like that someday."

"What did George Rogers do in the Northwest?" asked David.

"Haven't you heard?" exclaimed Peachy. "During the Revolutionary War the British held all the country northwest of the Ohio River as far as the Mississippi. They had forts in Illinois and Indiana and other places.

"George Rogers got about one hundred and fifty men to go with him. It was winter. The snow melted and covered the fields. The men had to go through water up to their waists.

"They surprised the British at Vincennes and captured a large force. Then they went on to seize two more forts. At the end of the war we held the whole Northwest Territory."

Meriwether thought, "This boy is strong and he has a nice face. His hair is the brightest red I have ever seen. He saved my life. The water would have pulled me down. Someday, if I can, I'll do something for him."

Midnight Adventure

COLD winter had come to the plantation. For miles around the country was drifted with snow. An icy wind blew down from the Ragged Mountains and tried to enter the Big House. It whistled at the windows and puffed in the chimneys. A stronger blast shook the windows of Meriwether's bedroom so hard they rattled.

Meriwether pulled the cover up to his chin and closed his eyes. It was a nice night to sleep.

Toward midnight the wind died down and a pale winter moon came out.

The two black-and-white hounds, Ponto and Lady, were sleeping in the kennel. They lay close together to keep warm. Their noses were on their paws. Suddenly Ponto woke up. He opened his eyes and looked at the bright night. In spite of the cold he wanted to be out. He stood up and walked to the door. Lady followed him into the yard.

A large red fox had passed through the yard a short time before. Ponto caught the scent and was off with his nose to the ground. Lady followed at his heels. Both dogs began to bark wildly as they ran.

Meriwether heard the noise and sat up in bed. Through the window he could see the dogs running across the white snow. He slipped out of bed and in no time at all was fully dressed.

A loose board in the hall creaked as he walked softly over it. The door of his mother's room opened. The boy waited.

"Merne, are you thinking of going out? It is so cold tonight and the snow is deep."

"Ponto and Lady are off. I'd like to see what they are chasing."

"Well, do be careful, and take Cuffy with you. So much could happen when you are out alone at night."

"I'll be careful, Mother."

Meriwether stopped in the pantry for some bread and meat. It was good to have a bit of food in one's pocket. He closed the house door behind him and whistled for Ruff.

Outside, the snow creaked under his boots. The bitter cold nipped the end of his nose. He turned toward the servants' quarters. There was no light in Cuffy's cabin. Cuffy did not like cold weather. He did not want to be an explorer as his master did. He would not enjoy going out into the night. He would go if Mister Merne asked him, though. Meriwether turned sharply away and started after the dogs. He would go by himself. Cuffy could sleep.

46

It was slow walking through the deep snow. The dogs had a head start. Still Meriwether kept on. It was easy to follow the trail in the bright moonlight. He wondered how far the hounds would go. If they were on the trail of a wise old fox, it might lead them a long chase.

Meriwether thought of his mother as he went along. How tall and pretty she was—and never afraid. No, he didn't think his mother was afraid of anything.

He remembered the time when some British officers had come to Locust Hill. At first they had been polite. Then one of them had asked, "What do you say, men, if we take over the house? It's more comfortable by far than our barracks. There are only a woman and some children here. We'll manage the workers. No one may come by here for weeks."

By this time Mrs. Lewis was on her feet. It was dark in the room but by the dancing firelight Meriwether saw her take the rifle from over the fireplace. She aimed it at the officers. Then she spoke. "The door is behind you! Open it and go at once! Never come here again! I warn you that I am a good shot."

Meriwether had run out of the room to call the servants. By the time he came back with Cuffy and Chloe, the officers were riding swiftly away down the drive. They never did come back.

Then there was the time when his father and some friends had gone deer hunting. They had left one morning when there was not even one piece of meat in the house for their dinner.

Chloe had thrown open the parlor door that afternoon and exclaimed, "Miss Lucy, I see a big deer in the yard!"

Mrs. Lewis had jumped and dropped her sewing. She took her rifle from the rack and went outside. She aimed, shot, and the deer fell. It was a large deer with great spreading antlers.

That evening the men came slowly back with empty hands. They had not seen even one deer. How surprised and pleased they were to see the big roast of venison steaming on the table!

Meriwether knew, too, that his aunts would never have let him go out exploring at night. His mother knew, though, that an explorer had to know about all kinds of weather.

Now the barking of the dogs was louder. The fox must have turned. Meriwether waited. It was quiet among the trees. Ruff growled and the hair rose on his neck. A scream came through the night.

"A panther!" exclaimed Meriwether. "Quiet, Ruff! It's in that tree."

The red fox was coming. The hounds were close behind him. Up in the tree the hungry panther lashed his tail and waited. Just as Ponto came below the tree the beast sprang.

The panther's sharp teeth bit into the dog's

neck. Ponto gave a yelp of pain. Ruff pulled at his collar. He wanted to get into the fight. Lady had already left the fox trail. Trying to help Ponto, she snapped at the panther.

"You stay out of this, Ruff! How can I shoot with all you dogs jumping around? Stay here!"

Ruff stood still, growling fiercely, while Meriwether ran over to where the two dogs and the panther were rolling about on the ground.

He placed his gun close to the panther's side and pulled the trigger. The beast gave one last snarl and then lay still.

Ponto lay quiet too. He had been badly hurt when the long claws dug into his back.

He could not walk. He lay on the cold snow. Meriwether knew that unless he helped Ponto, the poor dog would freeze before morning.

He must make a fire.

The young hunter's hand stole into his pocket. Yes, he was still carrying his precious tinderbox.

Under the roots of a pine tree he found dry twigs. Then he added a few larger pieces. In the tinderbox were flint and steel and bits of scorched linen. He struck the flint and steel together close to the linen. Sparks came and the linen began to smoke. He pushed the linen under the twigs and fanned it gently. The twigs burned. The warm fire made the woods bright.

Meriwether brought Ponto close to the fire. He found some pieces of bark and put under him. The dog lay very still. There was nothing more the boy could do.

In the morning someone would come.

All night the fire burned in the lonesome woods. Beside it sat a boy who kept awake in order to feed the fire. Sometimes he had to go long distances to find dry wood. He dragged branches back through the forest.

Lady whimpered and licked Ponto's sore back. Ruff sat close by Meriwether. Twice during the night the hair rose on his neck and he uttered a low growl. Two bright eyes shone in the darkness and then disappeared into the night. The watchful dog and the bright fire had driven the wild animals away.

In the morning Cuffy came looking for Meriwether. With him were four other servants. They carried Ponto back to the Big House. There Mrs. Lewis took care of his wounds.

"Mister Merne," said Cuffy, "why didn't you call me last night? Miss Lucy's plenty angry 'cause you went alone."

"I was going to call you, Cuffy, but you don't like to be cold. So I just went by myself."

"Mister Merne, next time you take me. Suppose a panther jumped on you!"

"All right, Cuffy. Next time I'll call you."

In two weeks Ponto could walk slowly about the yard. In two months he could run almost as fast and far as he had before he met the panther, but it was a long time before he and Lady started out again for a midnight ramble. When Ponto rose up to go, Lady would nip him sharply and Ponto would go back to his comfortable bed.

The winter was long and cold. Down in the servants' quarters all was not well. There was plenty of food and firewood but many of the servants were ill. Later on the illness spread from one to another.

It started one evening when Job tapped lightly on Meriwether's window. "Mister Merne," he whispered, "Chloe is sick and I don't know what to do. She can't seem to breathe and she aches all over."

"I'll come," the boy whispered. "You go back to Chloe. Build up the fire and put on a kettle of water. Hurry now!"

Meriwether dressed and then went to his mother's room. She was a light sleeper and she opened the door before he got there.

"What is it, Merne?"

"Job came. Chloe is ill. She has a hard time breathing and she aches all over."

"I'll go down to see as soon as I am dressed."

"Mother, you have not been well. Tell me what to do and I'll go down."

"Merne, nursing is woman's work. You come with me, though, so if I should be unable to go another time, you would know what to do. Please bring my medicine basket. There will be everything in it that I need."

Mrs. Lewis looked closely at Meriwether before she put on her cloak. "Merne, I'm going to give you a dose of this medicine before we go down to the quarters. Goodness knows what Chloe has, but I don't want you to catch it."

"How much?" asked Meriwether as he walked over toward the medicine basket.

"A large spoonful and don't scant it."

"I'll keep well just so I don't have to take

any more of that bitter stuff," he grumbled. "It tastes awful!"

"Jane really ought to be going along to learn about illness, but she has a slight cold and might catch a worse one. We will let her sleep," said Mrs. Lewis.

Meriwether took the basket and opened the rear door for his mother. The wind was high and snow blew around them as they made their way slowly through the drifts to reach the cabin.

Job's cabin was warm and the kettle was steaming over the fire.

"Good," said Mrs. Lewis. "Now, Chloe, you take this medicine while I soak this bark in some boiling water."

"Is Mister Merne there?" murmured Chloe.

"I'm here, Chloe. Take your medicine. Miss Lucy gave me some before we left the house."

"Then I'll take it," said Chloe, and she did.

"Is anyone else sick?" asked Mrs. Lewis.

"Yes, Miss Lucy," answered Job. "Cuffy aches all over, just like Chloe. There's no one in his cabin to care for him and the fire goes out."

"Now that I'm here with Chloe, you two go to Cuffy's cabin. Build up the fire and do for him as I am doing for Chloe. See that he takes his medicine and is warm. Later on I'll come along to see how he is."

It was late and the stars were dim in the sky when the two had finished making the two sick people comfortable.

"Mother, you don't look well yourself," said the boy. "You should take some of that bitter medicine and go to bed and stay there for a while. Jane can get breakfast."

"Very well," agreed Mrs. Lewis. "A few hours of rest and sleep are just the thing I need."

The illness swept through the quarters, but Meriwether knew what to do and could tell the well ones how to care for the sick.

"Where's Merne?" asked Uncle Frank when he rode over one day to see how they were getting on.

"Down in the quarters looking after the sick," answered Mrs. Lewis.

"Whatever is he doing there? It is no place for a child. First thing we know, he'll be down sick too."

"Well, Frank, what are we to do? I have been sick with a cold and so has Jane. Besides, even if you came to help, it would do no good. The servants will take medicine and directions only from Merne."

Uncle Frank gave a groan. "It is too much for a child, I say!"

"Perhaps so—but he is the only one who has kept well!"

Trouble at the Plantation

MERIWETHER held out a lump of sugar to Star, his bay mare. She nibbled it softly from the palm of his hand. After a gentle pat, he placed the saddle on her back. He quickly fastened the band to hold the saddle in place. Lem, the stableboy, looked on.

"Mister Merne, you sure do know how to put a saddle on a horse. That Star kicks at me every time I go near."

"You move too fast and frighten her. Come up from the side and speak before you touch her. She never kicks me."

"Sure enough, Mister Merne! You can gentle

all the horses—even that black villain yonder that we're all afraid of."

Meriwether glanced over at the stable yard where a big black horse was pawing the ground and tossing his head as he looked over the fence. "Well, yes. I keep an eye on him, though, just in case he may change his mind and try to bite me sometime."

Lem rolled his eyes and went back to cleaning the harness. Meriwether rode away toward the tobacco fields, where the servants were working. Bill Boyan, the white overseer, rode up and down on his horse, watching them.

There was something about the overseer that troubled the boy. Every since Bill Boyan had come to Locust Hill, the servants had seemed afraid. Before this they had liked to talk. Now they looked to see if Bill Boyan was near before they would answer a question. They no longer sang at their work or in their cabins at twilight.

Cuffy had even left the plantation—gone off in the night.

Meriwether thought again of his mother's anxious face as she had sat that morning going over the expense books of the plantation.

"There just isn't enough money to pay the bills, Merne," she had said. "I can't understand it. Your Uncle Nicholas does his very best, but he has his own plantation to look after and cannot spend all his time here. They tell me Cuffy is missing! Why should he want to run away? He has always wanted to do everything for you that he possibly could!"

Meriwether was on his way now to ask the field hands if they knew anything about Cuffy. As he drew near, Bill Boyan shouted to the workers, "Get on with your work and no talking!" Then to Meriwether he added in a gruff voice, "It takes too much time when they stop to talk to one another!"

Meriwether made no answer. He sat looking at the servants for a few moments. They said nothing. Now and then one of them glanced at him as if he were thinking of something he would like to say. At last Meriwether turned and rode slowly back to the house.

His sister Jane was in the cabin where the black women were weaving the coarse cloth that the field servants used for clothes. She had to spend part of each day there. Mrs. Lewis believed that her daughter should learn everything about a plantation home. Jane came out when her brother beckoned.

"Jane, where's Dilly?"

"In the kitchen, helping Chloe with the baking. Why?"

"Do you suppose she knows where Cuffy has gone?"

"I asked her. She says she doesn't, but perhaps she'll tell you more."

Chloe, plump, and always good-natured, welcomed him to the kitchen with a wide smile which showed all her white teeth. "Mister Merne always smells the ginger cookies baking," she said, taking the cover off the cookie crock, "and he's always nearly starved."

Meriwether bit slowly around the edge of a large cookie. "I want to talk to Dilly," he said to Chloe at last.

"Why do you want to talk to that silly girl, Mister Merne?"

"Cuffy's her brother. I want to ask her where he has gone."

"He's done run away."

"That's what everyone says. I think something must have frightened him. Cuffy has always liked it here at the plantation. I mean to find out what has happened to him to make him want to leave here."

Chloe seemed scared herself. "Mister Merne,

you're only a boy. Let Miss Lucy and Mister Nicholas take care of this."

"Uncle Nicholas is away in Richmond and Mother is busy. I want to know anything that you or Dilly have heard about Cuffy."

"I don't know anything, or Dilly either."

Dilly looked up from where she was beating

eggs in a wooden bowl. "Yes, I do too know something, Mister Merne."

Chloe turned angrily to the girl. "Shut your mouth, 'fore I cuff your ears! You want to get Mister Merne into trouble?"

Just at this moment Mrs. Lewis appeared in the open doorway, on her daily visit to the kitchen. She looked at their excited faces and asked, "What's the matter here?"

Meriwether asked, "Mother, am I not the owner of all Locust Hill?"

"Yes, Merne. You are the elder son, so all the eighteen hundred acres, the servants, and the house belong to you. Your Uncle Nicholas is your guardian and will manage for you until you are older. Why do you ask?"

"Mother, Dilly knows something about why Cuffy ran away, and Chloe won't let her tell me. If I own the plantation, don't I have the right to know what happens?"

"Miss Lucy," Chloe broke in, "I only want to keep that child out of trouble."

"True, Chloe, but if Master Merne wishes to know, it is his right to know. Tell us about Cuffy, Dilly."

Dilly twisted her hands in her apron but said not a word as she glanced sideways at Chloe.

Mrs. Lewis saw that the girl was afraid to talk. "Come into the office, Dilly. Chloe, Dilly is not to be scolded for anything she tells us. Whatever she knows may even help to make things better on the plantation."

When they reached the little room called the office, Mrs. Lewis said, "I'll wait in the hall to see that no one interrupts."

Dilly spoke in a frightened whisper. "Bill Boyan told Cuffy that he would have him sold down in the Carolina rice fields away from his family. Cuffy was afraid because he knew too much. So he ran away."

"What did he know?" Meriwether asked.

"Where the best tobacco went."

"Who took it?"

There was no answer.

"Dilly, you do know!" Meriwether persisted. "Was it Bill Boyan?"

The girl hesitated and looked again at the window before nodding her head.

"Where did Cuffy go? Into the mountains? To a cave?"

A look of terror came into the girl's face as she saw Bill Boyan ride into the yard. "I'm not saying any more, Mister Merne," she barely whispered. "I'm afraid."

"All right, Dilly. Thank you. Mother, will you come in now, please?"

When Mrs. Lewis heard the news, she exclaimed, "So that's where the trouble is! Only the other day the sheriff said that he did not trust Bill Boyan! A bad overseer can ruin the best plantation, and the servants are certainly afraid of him. What are we to do?"

"I'm going to the mountains to look for Cuffy. He'll be hungry."

"Merne, can't we wait until your Uncle Nicholas comes?"

"No, Mother. Cuffy may think what Bill Boyan said is really true unless I find him. You know it's my place to look after the servants."

"Then you'll need a lunch."

"Yes, a large one. Will Chloe fix it?"

"I'll pack the lunch myself. Merne, do be careful and try to be back as soon as possible. I'll be anxious."

A half-hour later, Meriwether set out for the mountains with his gun over his shoulder. His mother's heart was heavy as she watched him go, but Bill Boyan smiled to himself. He was glad to know that Meriwether would not be around to see what he was going to do that afternoon.

Since Meriwether often went away into the forests alone, it was no great surprise for the plantation folk to see him start off early that afternoon.

He took a path away from the mountains until he was out of sight. Then he circled back and began to climb upward. High on the mountainside was a deep cave where he and Cuffy had once taken shelter from a bad storm. The mouth of the cave was well hidden by thick bushes. It seemed the most likely place for the runaway to hide from Bill Boyan.

It was a hard climb up the mountainside. The long shadows made by the trees had disappeared. The woods were dim in the twilight when Meriwether came at last to the mouth of the cave. There was always the chance that a wildcat might be sleeping there, so he did not rush in.

He looked carefully on all sides to see if he had been followed. Then he walked into the dark cave and called out softly, "Cuffy, are you in there?"

There was a faint rustle in a pile of dry leaves in the back of the cave and a trembling voice said, "Is that you, Mister Merne? All alone? How come you knew where I went?"

"Yes, I'm all alone. Here's a lunch my mother sent you. Eat it and then we'll talk."

"Then Miss Lucy's not angry with me 'cause I ran away?"

"No. Eat your lunch."

Cuffy took a thick piece of bread in one hand and some ham in the other and ate with such large bites that in no time it was gone. More bread and meat soon followed it. Meriwether sat quietly on the ground near by and ate his lunch slowly and thoughtfully. When the last crumb had disappeared, Cuffy smacked his lips and gave a happy sigh. Then he began his story.

One day in town he had heard Bill Boyan

promise a strange man that he would sell him some tobacco.

Boyan would meet the man on a side road about a mile from Locust Hill next Tuesday.

Cuffy was surprised. He had always thought that only the folks at the Big House could sell the tobacco crop.

On Tuesday, when Bill Boyan drove away with the load, Cuffy slipped across the field and hid in the thick bushes by the roadside. He wanted to see what went on.

The stranger was waiting with two men and an empty wagon. He paid Bill Boyan and the tobacco was unloaded.

As Cuffy watched, Bill Boyan saw the bushes move. He stole up behind Cuffy and lashed his back with a whip.

"He had orders never to whip a servant!" exclaimed Meriwether.

"Lots of 'em get whipped hard when they don't

do what he says. He says he'll whip more if they tell on him, too."

"Well, I think he's going to have a surprise," Meriwether said angrily. "Cuffy, can you take a message from my mother to Uncle Nicholas Lewis at the Farm? If he is not at home, have my aunt send it on to Uncle Frank Meriwether. You are to stay on at the Farm and not come home until we send for you."

"There'll be moonlight tonight, Mister Merne, and I can find my way fine."

"All right then, be on your way and I'll start for home."

Cuffy finished his lunch and started to Uncle Nicholas' plantation.

It was late when Meriwether arrived at Locust Hill, but his mother was up and waiting for him.

"Did you have good hunting?" she asked. As soon as the servant had left the room, she said, "Now tell me all about it."

Two days later Mr. Nicholas Lewis, Mr. Frank Meriwether, Mr. Thomas Jefferson, and Captain Marks, who was the sheriff of Albemarle County, came riding up the long driveway to the Big House.

Company came often, but seldom so many important people at one time. The Big House and the servants' quarters buzzed with talk. The house servants hurried about. Job was sent to bring Bill Boyan to the Big House.

The overseer walked into the house with a swaggering stride. He came out a very surprised man. The sheriff's hand was on his arm. Captain Marks took him away to town. No one at Locust Hill ever saw him again. That night there were laughter and singing once again in the servants' quarters.

A few days afterward Uncle Nicholas, Uncle Frank, Mr. Jefferson, and Captain Marks came again and talked with Mrs. Lewis.

"You should not be without a man on the place," said Uncle Frank.

"Your son should not have so much to do," said Uncle Nicholas.

"We all know that. Surely you didn't ride over just to tell me this," Mrs. Lewis said, as she smiled at Captain Marks.

"Well, the truth is, I asked them to come along with me," said Captain Marks slowly. "I came to ask you to marry me!"

Mrs. Lewis gave a little gasp and sat down quickly. It was some time before she said quietly and thoughtfully, "Brother Frank, what do you think of this idea?"

"I think you should marry again. It's a very good idea," he answered.

"What is your opinion, Nicholas?"

"Well, as the children's guardian, I can say that I would feel much better if there were a man on the place—especially if it were someone we know as a good neighbor and true friend. After all, though, Jane and Meriwether are old enough to say how they feel about it too. Next to you, they are the ones most concerned. Meriwether, please go and ask Jane to come here," said Nicholas Lewis.

Jane was in the garden with her cousin Edmund Anderson. She was cutting beautiful red roses with long stems and putting them into a basket. When her brother told her why she had been sent for, Jane did not seem surprised in the least.

"We might as well say yes," she said thoughtfully. "Mother is still young and is sure to marry again sometime, I suppose. Captain Marks has been calling for months and he is very nice. I'd be glad to have her marry him."

In the large parlor the grown people were waiting for them. Jane and Meriwether came and stood in the doorway.

"Come in, children," said Mrs. Lewis. "Jane, do you know why we sent for you?"

"Yes, Mother. I think that it would be fine for you to marry Captain Marks."

"What do you say, Merne?"

Meriwether stood quietly for a moment without speaking. He was thinking of his soldier father in the blue and buff uniform and of the good times they had had when he was home on leave. He could never like any man so much as Father—or so much as Uncle Nicholas either. Captain Marks was very good company, though, and he always had time to talk to a boy. Besides, Mother liked him.

"It will be all right, Mother."

"Thank you, son."

Jane and Meriwether then slipped away into the garden.

"It means a wedding and there'll be lots of company," said Jane. "All the relatives will come. The house will be filled. We'll have to have new clothes. I hope to have a lovely yellow silk dress for the occasion."

Meriwether listened without saying anything. He was hoping that the wedding would bring some of their cousins who lived many miles away. There were always good times when they came to Locust Hill.

The Trader

NIGHT HUNG OVER Locust Hill. Down in the servants' quarters everyone was sleeping. In the Big House there was not even one light.

Meriwether lay sound asleep. He was dreaming of a trader's pack train going on and on in single file toward the unknown West. A wise old gray mare was leading the way. The bell on her neck rang slowly as she walked. He awoke, and the bell was still ringing. It was under the window.

He rubbed his eyes, sprang out of bed and ran to look out. There below, in the moonlight, were some pack horses. They were standing around the front door. A large figure sat motionless on a tired horse whose drooping head almost touched the ground.

Meriwether pulled on some clothes and ran down the hall to rap on his mother's door.

When she answered, he said, "There's someone at the door. In the moonlight it looks like Trader Jones, the man Uncle Nicholas and I met at Michie Tavern. Something seems to be wrong with him."

His mother was soon beside him with a rifle in her hand. "Open the door, Merne."

The heavy front door swung open and Mrs. Lewis and Meriwether stepped outside into the chilly night. The trader swayed in the saddle and spoke in a low voice. "I had a fight with some wandering Chickasaws—days ago—beyond the mountains. They tried to drive off the pack horses. I finally got away, but they put an arrow in my back. I couldn't get it out and I'm burning up with fever. I've always heard, Mistress Lewis, that you have skill in medicine and are willing to nurse the sick. Can you do anything to stop my pain?"

The sound of the bell had awakened some of the house servants. They came slowly around the corner with lanterns in their hands.

Mrs. Lewis said firmly, "Cuffy and Chloe, help the sick man down and into the house. Put him on the couch in the office. Merne, see that the packs are removed from the animals and put in the storeroom for safety. Then turn the horses into the stable yard for the night with plenty of feed and water."

The pack horses could hardly lift their feet from the ground to follow the gray mare when Meriwether led her away toward the storehouse. There he took off the heavy packs and stowed them carefully away in the log house. Then he locked the door with a big key. He put the key

back into his pocket and led the horses into the stable yard.

Meriwether filled the big trough with water and set out food, but although the hungry animals drank some of the water they were much too tired to eat. He left them standing with drooping heads in the yard.

By the time he went back to the house, Mrs. Lewis had the arrow out of the trader's back and was bathing the sore spot with cool water. "No poison," she said, when Meriwether looked at the arrow and the wound. "With care I think this good man will recover."

Meriwether and his mother put Trader Jones to bed. Chloe started a wood fire in the kitchen fireplace. She heated broth for the sick man. He drank it and said, "More, please. It's a long time since I've eaten, Mistress Lewis."

"That is enough for now," answered Mrs. Lewis. "There will be more in the morning.

Now rest and try to go to sleep. This salve will heal your back."

The trader lay down and closed his eyes. Everything was still. In a moment he would be fast asleep.

All at once there was the sharp clang of a bell. Then came the sound of horses' feet. They were running.

Meriwether started for the door to see what was happening. He stopped when Trader Jones tried to sit up and cried out, "No! No! Stay here! Someone is driving off my horses! He may shoot! Put out the light!"

Mrs. Lewis snuffed out the candle and the room was left in darkness.

In the moonlight they could see the outline of two men on horseback lashing the horses down the driveway.

"They won't go far," murmured the trader. "It's the packs they're after."

"The packs are safe in the storeroom," said Meriwether.

"Good boy!" murmured the man as he sank back on the pillow. Soon he fell asleep.

In the morning a searching party from the plantation found the horses in a field not far away where the thieves had left them.

Trader Jones's eyes shone when he heard the good news. "It was some of the Chickasaws who kept on my trail even here to your door," he said. "I'm glad no trouble came to this house because you took me in.

"The Indians you saw were looking for furs," he explained. "They knew my packs were full. Spring came early this year. I was the first to trade with the Shawnees. The young men had been hunting during the winter. They had some fine skins.

"I gave them blankets, red cloth, and some kettles. They gave me skins. Then I started for

84

home. The pack horses could not hurry, for the packs were too heavy. Then the Chickasaws crossed my trail.

"The Indians came up behind me at a bend in the trail. They shot many arrows. You saw the one in my back. I got the horses safely around the bend, and then I turned to face the Indians. I had to use my gun. Some of the Indians fell. The others ran back.

"I got the horses going again. We went on hour after hour and day after day. Someone was always pursuing me. I went on and on. The way was long and rough. It is good to be here. Now I shall get well.

"The Chickasaws will not come back. They'll expect every man in Albemarle to be out after them. We can sleep tonight."

He was right. No one in Albemarle ever caught sight of them again. They just vanished into the forest.

Trader Jones lay in bed for many days. Slowly he grew better. One day he sat in a chair by the window. The next day he walked up and down the room. Soon he would be leaving.

One evening Jane said, "Trader Jones, does anything funny ever happen on the trail?"

The man thought for a while. Then he laughed and said, "This story is about the time I surprised a bear—and myself too.

"It was a few years ago in the springtime. I was coming home with packs of furs. Some friendly Shawnees came along the trail. They said bad Indians were waiting on the valley trail ahead of me.

"It would be dangerous if I turned back the way I had come. The bad Indians could catch up with me. The first thing I had to do was to wrap cloth around the mare's bell. Then I started the horses up the mountainside on a secret trail. The trail was very steep and narrow. The mare led the way as usual. I rode in the rear. All at once the mare stopped short. I knew there was something wrong. I got off my horse and walked forward past the pack animals."

"What was it?" asked Jane.

"A big black bear! He was standing on the trail in front of the mare. The horses were beginning to back. They were near the edge then. A little farther and down would go both horses and all of my furs!"

"Whatever did you do?" asked Meriwether.

"I didn't dare shoot. A shot would bring up the Indians from below.

"Just then the bear growled and started for the mare.

"That mare is a good animal and she has been with me a long time. I ran toward the bear. I was going to hit him with my rifle, for I thought it might scare him away. The path went downhill. When I was almost up to the bear my foot caught in the root of a tree. Over I went and fell right against Mr. Bear headfirst. I saw stars, and Mr. Bear got a big bump. It upset him. He went over backward off the trail and rolled over and over down the mountain.

"The horses were scared. Bears always frighten horses, you know. Too, at any moment the bear might come back. They wanted to run. I led the mare until we were far away from the place. We went quickly over the mountain and slowly down the other side.

"There we came to a camp of friendly Indians. Around the campfire I told them the bear story. They laughed and laughed and named me Big Bear Hunter."

Now Jane laughed too. She felt that her question was answered.

The next morning was fine. Trader Jones looked out the window and said, "Today I must go. First, Mistress Lewis, I give my best skins—

beaver, marten, or mink—to you for what you have done for me."

Mrs. Lewis shook her head. "Thank you, Trader Jones. You were our guest. A guest does not pay. We are glad indeed that you came to us. Come soon again."

That day Trader Jones rode away. He was quite well again and eager to be out on the trails.

After he had finished trading his furs at Williamsburg he would turn once more toward the Indian villages.

Thomas Jefferson to the Rescue

ONE DAY a messenger rode from the main road up the long driveway that led to Locust Hill. He handed Mrs. Lewis a letter. As she read it her face turned pale.

"Is it bad news, Mother?" asked Meriwether anxiously.

"Yes, it's very bad news. When your father and I were married, your Grandfather Meriwether gave me fourteen hundred acres of land for a wedding gift. For several years after that his tobacco crop was poor. When he died and his other lands were sold there was not enough money to pay all the debts. Now the men to whom he owed money wish to take away my fourteen hundred acres."

"Mother, that's not right. You don't owe them any money."

"True, my son, but those men have brought suit to get the land. The case will go into court and be heard before a judge. If we do not have a good lawyer who can explain that my land was given to me before your grandfather's crops failed, we may lose it. The good lawyers are far away in Williamsburg, though."

"Isn't our neighbor, Thomas Jefferson, a lawyer, Mother?"

"Why, of course he is, and a very fine one too! I forgot, because he has been away from Albemarle County so much—first in Philadelphia and then as governor. I'm sure that he would be willing to help with this case if he has time. I'll send you over right now to ask him. Saddle your horse while I write a note."

Some time later Meriwether rode up the steep mountain road that led to the Jefferson home on the rounded mountaintop. On any other day Meriwether might have stopped to look down at the wide forests and green fields which lay far below. Now he was thinking about his mother's affairs. He rode along without even looking at the little town of Charlottesville in the valley.

He came up to the large house in the middle of a green lawn. It was a beautiful house built of red brick with white wood trim and a dome which shone in the clear air. Mr. Jefferson had made the plans for the house himself and loved the place dearly. He called it Monticello, which means "Little Mountain."

A stableboy came running to take Meriwether's horse. Visitors were always welcome at Mr. Jefferson's home.

Meriwether went up to the east portico. He liked to look at the large clock which was high up on the wall. It had one clock face on the outside wall and another clock face inside the house. Every Sunday the clock was wound by cannon balls which hung on weights.

A weather vane was set above the east portico and it turned with the wind. On the ceiling of the room below was an indicator which showed the direction of the wind.

Meriwether wished that he had time to go through the long passageways beneath the house. Off the passageways were the rooms for the servants, the blacksmith shop, and many others. There was even a long passage which led to the stables. This was so the servants did not have to go outside the house in bad weather. Even the kitchen was in the cellar.

On most plantations such rooms were usually found back of the big house.

By the time Meriwether reached the wide front door, a servant was there to open it.

Meriwether waited in the study where there were many books. He had good manners and did not touch anything, but just looked around.

From where he stood he could look through the alcove where Mr. Jefferson's bed was placed. Mr. Jefferson smiled as he looked at the boy's puzzled face.

"You see," he explained, "if I think of something during the night that should be written down at once, it is easy to get out of bed on the study side and write it down. When it's time for breakfast, I get out on the bedroom side and get dressed in a hurry.

"Come on in the library, my boy," Mr. Jefferson said with a smile, when they reached the door of the library. "Come in and see what I'm working on. It's a writing desk. It is not very big, but it will hold everything I need when writing letters."

Meriwether handed Mr. Jefferson his mother's

letter and walked over to see the small writing desk which sat on the table. It was a pretty little desk complete with goose quills, ink, paper, and wax. When the paper was folded the wax was used to seal it.

On a visit to Monticello it was always interesting to look around and see what Mr. Jefferson had made. There was always something new.

Meriwether stood for a while longer at the windows. He looked down now at the beautiful valley. Then he turned anxiously to Mr. Jefferson, who sat thinking about the letter.

At last the good neighbor said, "Tell your mother that I'll be glad to take the case. The land belongs to her and we'll try to make the court see it that way."

A few weeks later the land case came up in court. Mr. Jefferson was there as Mrs. Lewis' lawyer and he pleaded the case so well that the judge decided she should keep all her land.

The Secret

IT WAS about this time that Meriwether had a secret all his own.

Far away from the Big House stood an old shed. The secret was in there. It was three little baby skunks!

Meriwether had found them in the forest. The mother skunk was dead, and the babies were crying in a hollow stump. The boy peeped in at them. They were pretty little things. Too bad they must soon die!

Meriwether touched one. Its fur was soft. He turned toward home, then came back. All three skunks went into his pocket.

97

They cried softly all the way home. Meriwether put them in the shed and locked the door. Then he went to the kitchen and asked Chloe for some bread and milk.

"What are you feeding now?" asked Chloe.

"It's a secret," said Meriwether. "Every day I want a dish of bread and milk."

"Just some no-count animal again," grumbled Chloe as she gave him the dish.

The little skunks grew rapidly. Their fur was long, black, and glossy. They had wide white stripes down their backs. They walked proudly with tails high in the air. Each day they waited for Meriwether to bring their food. When he was late they scratched on the floor or thumped loudly with their feet.

One day Mrs. Lewis sent Cuffy to find Meriwether. Cuffy came to the shed but went no farther than the doorway. What he saw made him jump back.

"Come away!" he exclaimed. "Skunks are bad! Miss Lucy won't like it!"

Cuffy could never keep a secret, so Meriwether had to tell his mother about the new pets.

Mrs. Lewis was angry. "Whatever is the matter with you, Merne? Bringing skunks in from the woods, indeed! We have more than enough around here now. Wait until they turn on you someday. You'll have to bury your clothes and stay out of the house for a week. You had better get rid of them right away."

"I'd like to keep them a little while longer, Mother. When they're older I'll take them away to the woods."

"Very well, then, if you must," said his mother, "but I'm afraid you'll be sorry!"

The next day Mrs. Lewis' cousin Sue came for a long visit. She brought her son Herbert with her. Herbert was ten years old. He was never still except when he slept.

Things began to happen after Herbert arrived. He chased the cows just to see them run. Then the cows did not give much milk because they had been frightened.

Herbert started the dogs fighting. He sent chickens flying off their nests. When Meriwether told him to stop his pranks, Herbert ran to tell his mother. Cousin Sue did not like to have Herbert scolded.

Meriwether spoke to his mother. "Herbert's going to get hurt," he said. "Today I found him hitting Star with a whip. I took the whip away and sent him out of the stable. Star will kick Master Herbert if he doesn't stay away."

Mrs. Lewis sighed. "Cousin Sue invited herself for this visit. She may stay for months. We've had nothing but trouble since that boy came. The servants don't like him and he upsets the house. Do keep an eye on him, Merne, so that nothing terrible will happen."

One day Meriwether was kept so busy stopping Herbert from hurting the animals and tearing up flowers and vegetables from the garden that he had no time to feed the little skunks.

It was late in the afternoon when he finally arrived with their pan of bread and milk. When he opened the door, no fluffy pets came to greet him. All was quiet. Meriwether was not only surprised but anxious.

He looked behind the spades and shovels. He looked behind the rakes and hoes. There was no sign of the pets. They just were not there!

However, in a corner behind the rakes there was a rat hole that was perhaps big enough for the little skunks to slip through. To prove this, there were two glossy black hairs caught on the rough board.

The three must have gone out that way.

First of all, Meriwether found some nails and a thick board. He nailed the board over the rat hole. Then he started out to look for the run-away skunks.

Where would they be likely to go? To his mother's strawberry patch, of course! There the berries were rosy red and ripe enough for jam and jelly. They were to be picked the next day.

There was a tightly woven fence around the strawberry patch, but this had not kept the skunks out. They had crawled underneath. They were wandering about among the berries, taking a bite from one and then another—always seeming to think the next berry would be better.

Meriwether hoped Chloe and Dilly would not notice this when they came to pick the berries the next day. His mother would be angry if she heard about it.

At Meriwether's whistle the smallest skunk came toward him and the others soon followed. As they reached the fence, they waited to be picked up. They made little noises of pleasure at

seeing him. Meriwether laughed. "You are really too big to be carried," he exclaimed.

He picked them up and carried them in his arms, though. "You would make nice pets if it wasn't for the odor," he said as he stroked their fur. "I suppose you will have to go back to the woods. I'll find you a nice place."

When they reached the shed all three began at once to eat their bread and milk. They ate noisily, and while they were doing this the boy slipped quietly away, closing and locking the door behind him.

A couple of days later Herbert threw stones at Ruff and pulled feathers out of the rooster's tail. Then he ran into the orchard. He saw the shed where the skunks were. Meriwether had forgotten to lock the door.

Herbert went inside. The skunks came to meet him. The only human being they knew was Meriwether, and he was kind. Herbert did not know they were skunks. He thought they were kittens and pulled their tails hard.

The skunks grew angry. They threw an ill-smelling liquid all over him. It blinded the boy. He came screaming out of the shed and ran up to the house.

Mrs. Lewis met the boy at the door. "Stay out! Don't come in here!" she exclaimed. "Go to the woodshed and take off your clothes. Chloe will bring some water for a bath."

Herbert's mother came. "What has happened? Oh, how terrible! My poor boy! Are you keeping him out of the house?" she cried.

"Yes, indeed," answered Mrs. Lewis. "Merne would have to stay out if it had happened to him. We can't have that odor in here."

"Very well then," said Cousin Sue crossly. "Herbert, go and change your clothes. We will leave a house in which we are not welcome. We will go this very afternoon."

Cuffy buried the clothes in the field. Herbert and his mother drove away within the hour.

Meriwether said, "I'm very sorry, Mother. Now that the harm's done, I'll take the skunks back to the woods."

His mother looked angry. Then she laughed. "It was terrible, but I'm not sorry that boy has gone. Keep your pets if you wish, but keep them away from me."

That evening Meriwether took the pan of bread and milk to the shed as usual. He talked kindly and the three pets willingly followed him far up to the field. He gave them the food and left them there. They were big enough now to care for themselves.

A Wedding at Locust Hill

Jane got her new silk dress, but she was disappointed to learn that her mother did not plan to have a large wedding.

"No, indeed, Jane," said Mrs. Lewis firmly. "Such a wedding is not for me. I am a widow and should have only a small, quiet wedding. Then, too, we Meriwethers do not believe in much fuss and fashion."

Mrs. Lewis and Captain Marks were married with only the near relatives and a few folks from near-by Albemarle plantations invited.

Still, as Mrs. Lewis had ten brothers and sisters, who came with their families, it made quite a houseful. When Uncle Nicholas and many of his brothers and sisters arrived with their families, the large rooms were crowded to the doors.

Last of all came Mr. Thomas Jefferson to see his neighbors married.

The kitchen had been full of spicy odors for days. Fruitcakes, cookies, and meat pies stood on the shelves. Chloe had made a large wedding cake and covered it with white icing. This stood in the center of the dining-room table. Around it were large platters of venison, turkey, and ham. Near by were plates of beaten biscuit.

There were far too many people for all to be seated at the table. So they sat in little groups talking and laughing. It was a happy gathering. The small children sat on the stairs. They were in the way of everyone going up or down, but they could see what went on below.

The servants were kept busy passing plates of food and cups of tea and coffee.

Jane was a very busy person. She wanted everything to go well at her mother's wedding. She went from the dining room to the kitchen and back again. Edmund Anderson was often at her side.

Captain Marks had business in Williamsburg and thought it would be a good time to take a trip there. He and Mrs. Marks drove away in the middle of the afternoon. This left Jane in charge of the house.

Early next morning, while Jane was busy seeing that the house was cleaned, Meriwether went down to the river. He knew a quiet pool where trout darted about and it seemed a good day to catch several. Once there, though, he completely forgot about trout fishing, for Will Clark was sitting on the bank.

"Hello!" exclaimed Meriwether. "Where have you been? Everyone I asked said you lived over east in Caroline County."

"That's where we live," answered Will Clark. "I was born there. I was here on a visit with my mother before—at the time you were lost in the cave. Now we are visiting some cousins before we move out to Kentucky. My brother George Rogers has a place for us there, near Louisville—a big house with servants and acres of land. It's called Mulberry Hill. It will be the first nice place we've ever owned."

"That's a long way off. When will you be back here again?" asked Meriwether.

"Perhaps never. George Rogers likes the new country. He says there is a chance there for poor people, so we'll stay. Perhaps sometime you'll come out to Kentucky to visit us," said Will.

"I've wanted to see what lies over the mountains ever since Trader Jones told his stories. Someday I'll find out. You will see it all first."

"George Rogers says it would take years to see everything. There'll be plenty left for you."

110

The boys talked of hunting and fishing and the sun was soon high in the sky.

"It's noon and that means mealtime. Let's go home!" exclaimed Meriwether.

Jane was glad when the two boys came to eat with Reuben and her. The four of them laughed and talked at the table while they ate Chloe's good cooking.

In the afternoon the boys looked at the horses and went for a walk through the fields. Before long the sun was low in the west and the trees cast long shadows.

"I must go," said Will. "We will leave early in the morning."

Then he held out his hand. In it was a small, round, white and yellow stone. "I'd like to give you my lucky stone," he said.

Meriwether's hand closed firmly over it. He liked stones and this one was different. It might bring luck, but, best of all, Will Clark had given it to him. What could he give his friend in return? His hand went into his pocket and came out with the left hind foot of a rabbit which Cuffy had given him only the week before.

"Cuffy says a rabbit's foot is always lucky," he said. "Take it with you for good luck on your trip out to Kentucky."

Then Meriwether watched the older boy go

down the hillside and out of sight. Then he went back to Locust Hill.

He had promised his mother to stay near the house all the time while she was away, in case Jane might need him.

Cuffy was just starting out to look for him. "Come quick, Mister Merne!" he exclaimed. "That Jody who drives the tobacco wagon has cut his leg. It's hurt bad. He kicks hard when Miss Jane tries to fix it. She said for you to come and hold his legs."

The cut was deep. By the time Jane had it bandaged, dinner was ready.

Then there was a new colt in the stable to be looked after and a quarrel between two of the field servants to settle.

Meriwether was so tired that he fell asleep as soon as his head touched the pillow. By the time he awoke in the morning, Will Clark was well on his way to Kentucky.

Journey to
Georgia

A YEAR passed quickly. Captain Marks was well liked by the three Lewis children. The servants liked him too, but they still took their troubles to Meriwether.

One day a baby, little John Marks, was born at the Big House.

After that Captain Marks was not happy to live on at Locust Hill. He wanted a plantation of his very own for his small son.

Then Uncle Frank Meriwether came to Locust Hill with exciting news. In faraway Georgia there were acres and acres of rich land to be had for very little money. He and Uncle Thomas

Gilmer were taking a group of men and their families to live there. They would make a settlement on the banks of the Broad River.

Uncle Frank asked his sister and Captain Marks to go with them. Captain Marks thought it was a fine idea. Mrs. Marks did not think so well of the plan. She raised several objections. Meriwether listened closely to the talk from where he lay on the rug in front of the fireplace playing with the baby.

"It's a long, long way from home," said Mrs. Marks slowly.

"It's a chance to take up some rich new land," said her brother.

"It's a chance for me to start a new plantation for little John," said Captain Marks.

"What about Merne?" asked Mrs. Marks anxiously. "He couldn't stay alone here at Locust Hill while we are so far away."

"Why not take him along with us? The boy

likes to explore and it would be a chance for him to see the country," said Captain Marks. "You could teach him for another year or two until he comes back here to go to school."

"What about the plantation? It will soon grow up in weeds if there is no one to look after it!" exclaimed Mrs. Marks.

"I'm sure that Nicholas Lewis will look after things here while the boy's away," said Frank Meriwether. "With a good overseer and the servants still on the place, the plantation could be kept going until Merne is old enough to take charge himself."

"Jane will not want to go to Georgia! She is engaged to her cousin Edmund Anderson," said her mother. "They told me about it only this morning."

"Well, if Jane is engaged, I think there will soon be another wedding at Locust Hill," said Captain Marks.

No, Jane did not wish to go to Georgia. She decided to be married and stay in Virginia.

Jane had a big chest full of table linen, bed linen, and towels. Some of the things had been given to her when she was still very young.

Now she had to have a wedding dress and many other new clothes. Everything had to be made at home.

Some of the aunts and older girl cousins came to stay. They helped Jane and her mother sew. It was weeks before everything was finished.

Then one day when the cakes were baked, the meat was roasted, and the wedding dress ready, Jane and Edmund were married.

Jane was a lovely bride. She wore a pretty white silk dress. Many people were at the wedding. It kept Mrs. Marks and the aunts busy seeing that all the guests had plenty of good things to eat.

Jane was a very young bride—only fifteen

years old—but already she knew how to manage a plantation home very well.

After the wedding Jane went with her husband to live in Louisa County. It took more than a day's ride to get there.

Mrs. Marks was a wise woman. She did not like to leave her comfortable home, but when she saw that her husband's mind was set on going to Georgia, she said no more.

For many days after the wedding the house servants hurried about their work. They had never moved so fast before. There was much to do. The rooms had to be cleaned and many things stored away. There were trunks and boxes to pack. Food that would keep had to be cooked for the journey, and the Big House had to be closed.

The other families who were going in the party to Georgia were kept waiting until the Markses were ready to leave.

Most of the servants would stay behind at Locust Hill. Chloe, however, would go along to cook for the family, Dilly to care for little John, and Cuffy to be with his Mister Merne. The other servants who were going along all belonged to Captain Marks.

Everyone ran here and there looking for this and that. It seemed to the waiting Captain Marks as if the work would never end.

Every day Captain Marks said, "How soon will you be ready?"

Every day Mrs. Marks answered, "Not yet. There is so much to do."

One day Captain Marks did not ask. That evening as the family was at dinner Mrs. Marks said, "Everything is ready. Tomorrow we can begin our journey."

The children clapped their hands happily.

Captain Marks exclaimed, "I can't believe it! Ready at last! I thought we would never get away. We must go to sleep early tonight so we can make a good start in the morning."

The next day everyone was up with the sun.

The servants carried the bags, boxes, and trunks out of the house and piled them in the covered wagons. The wagons were filled to the top with things which would be needed on the new plantation. There were farm tools, feed for the horses, and even chickens in crates.

At last all the windows of the Big House were closed and the doors locked.

Captain Marks gave the word to start. The horses began to trot, and the family and servants were off on the long journey to a new home in the backwoods of Georgia.

At the start of the journey Captain Marks, Meriwether, and Reuben were the only happy people in the Locust Hill party. To them it was fun to go on such a long trip. Mrs. Marks was very sad. She had tears in her eyes as she looked back at the comfortable home she was leaving. The servants had long, unhappy faces. Georgia was far away. They were leaving their cabins and their friends. They were afraid of what might happen in the far-off land.

Many uncles, aunts, and cousins were leaving Virginia. The plantation land was worn out. Too many crops had been planted on it, and no fertilizer had been used. They were all going to Georgia to make new homes.

Uncle Frank Meriwether was waiting for the Locust Hill party at the crossroads.

"Well! Well!" he exclaimed as he rode up. "Here you are at last! Another day and we would have had to go on without you! The Gilmer and McGehee families are already well on the way."

Everyone knew that Uncle Frank was joking. He had promised to wait for them and he would.

Captain Marks and Meriwether helped to get

the wagon train in order. Then the word was given to start and off they went.

The long line of wagons went slowly over the rough road. Ruff was busy running about to see that everything was all right. Zeke Brown, a white overseer, was in charge of Captain Marks's wagons. Behind the wagons came the cattle. Sometimes the servants rode and sometimes they walked along to watch the cattle and keep them from straying away.

At noon the travelers stopped to have lunch and to rest the animals. By this time Ruff was so tired that he was glad to lie down. He was no longer a young dog. That afternoon he rode in a wagon. He slept most of the time but always with one eye open.

In late afternoon the next stop was made on the banks of a large creek. It was time to make camp for the night. First the servants took water from the creek for drinking. Then the horses drank. Later the cattle waded into the stream and took long drinks while the water cooled their tired feet. After a good meal, the weary travelers slept in the wagons.

Each day the travelers went a few more miles. Each morning they awoke in a different place. Every day brought new sights.

Travel went smoothly over the level ground, but when the wagon train came to a river or creek it had to stop. This was because there were few bridges along the way.

When the wagon train stopped, the men would look for a good place to cross. There had to be a hard bottom in the creek or river. The water must be low.

Captain Marks and Uncle Frank would ride their horses into the water. The wagons followed far apart. They did this so that if any of the horses slipped and fell on the wet stones there would be room for them to get up again.

Meriwether and other boys brought up the rear, riding behind the cattle. What a noise the cattle made when they hit the water! The cows mooed loudly and the boys shouted to keep them moving along.

On the other side there would be a steep climb up the banks, and after that a stop to rest.

The travelers made camp at night when they grew tired. The young cousins had good times in the evenings. If the camp was made near a river the boys often went swimming. After supper both the boys and girls sang around the campfire. Sometimes they played games by the light of the moon and used the tree trunks for hiding places.

When the children played games Meriwether was at his best. Sometimes they played Old Gray Wolf. Then Meriwether came so quietly through the twilight that he was often at a child's side before he was noticed. The thought of a wolf could become very real when it grew dark. Sometimes when old Ruff, who was kind and gentle, nosed a small player's hand, the child would let out a yell. Then the other children laughed at the joke.

In another group the servants sang hymns while they rested after the day's journey.

The little party traveled slowly because of the livestock. The cows could not hurry. Their feet got sore when they walked too far. The cows did not want to go away from the home meadows. At night they had to be watched to keep them from starting back toward home.

At first the travelers met friends along the way. The farther they went the fewer people they met. The big plantations were soon past as they went on down toward North Carolina.

One evening it was raining. It was a cold heavy rain. They came at last to a small tavern. Here they stopped, for Captain Marks said it would be better for his party to be inside for the night. Little John Marks had a bad cold.

The women and children had the one big room upstairs, while the men slept in front of the fireplace on the floor below. Morning came and after a good breakfast they all felt better, except little John. He had grown worse during the night, so they made a late start.

Captain Marks's overseer had the wagons in place and the livestock moving by the time the family was ready to go. The rest of the party had gone on ahead.

At this moment some friends of Captain Marks rode up to the tavern.

"We heard you were here," said one man. "Can you wait? Joel Brown is coming and wants to see you before you head into the wilderness."

"I can wait for a while but not long," said Captain Marks. "You can see that the stock is already on the way."

It was decided that Mrs. Marks should ride on in the carriage with Reuben and little John and overtake the others.

When Mrs. Marks finally caught up with the Locust Hill wagons, it was to find something wrong. They had stopped.

"What's the trouble?" she asked.

"Mr. Zeke is sick," said Cuffy. "There's no one to tell the new servant folks what to do."

Mrs. Marks walked over to the wagon where the overseer lay. He was really too ill to drive or give orders. Mrs. Marks had to take charge.

While Dilly took care of small John, Mrs. Marks rode up and down the wagon train and got it started again. When anyone could not manage a team of lively horses, she herself took the reins and drove.

At noon they overtook the main wagon train.

All the uncles and aunts came to see what had been the matter.

"Where have you been?"

"Where is Captain Marks?"

"Why are you driving?" asked the women.

"We would have come back to help you," said the men.

"It's good to get here. My arms are certainly tired," said Mrs. Marks.

It was not until the next day that Captain Marks caught up with them. His friend had owed him some money, and he had waited, hoping that at last it was going to be paid. The friend had failed to bring the money, though.

As they went on all was not sunshine and laughter and games. There were days when it rained. There were long pulls up the mountains that tired the horses. Then there was the going down again with brakes set on the rear wheels to keep the wagons from pushing the horses headlong down the hill.

After weeks of slow travel everyone was very

weary. The men were most anxious to get to Georgia and start work on the plantations. They talked very little.

The women were tired of meals cooked over campfires. Even the children were cross. They had been on the way too long.

At last one sunny afternoon the travelers came to the end of their journey. The wagon train rolled to a stop on the banks of the Broad River. It was here that the settlement was to be made. The ground was low. There was not a house in sight. It was not a cheerful place. The Georgia pine woods were close and dark. Still everyone was glad they had arrived.

"Well," said Mrs. Marks as she looked about her, "this is certainly wild country."

"Yes, it is wild," agreed Captain Marks, "but it won't always be like this. The soil is rich and the climate is warm. In a few years we'll have a fine plantation going. You wait and see."

"I shall wait," said Mrs. Marks. "What about a house to live in now, though?"

"We'll start cutting trees tomorrow. In a few days the house will be up. It will be only a small one at first. Later on we can add on to it. Meanwhile we'll sleep in the wagons. Have Chloe cook something for us to eat now. Then we'll turn in, so that we can be all ready to begin our new life in the morning."

Cherokee Trouble

THE SETTLERS along the Broad River were worried. All day they had turned their heads to look anxiously toward the deep woods which ran not far from their plantations. Word had come that the Cherokees and Creeks were on the warpath. The Indians were angry because the white men were taking over their hunting grounds. When trees were cut down the wild animals disappeared. Hunting was poor and the Indians went hungry. Now they were going to drive the white settlers from Georgia. Then it would be their own land again.

One day a settler from a farm down the river

ran into the Virginia settlement. "The Cherokees are coming!" he gasped. "They are headed this way! They burned our cabin while I was in the fields! Then they took my wife and children as their prisoners!"

By the time he had finished speaking every man and boy had reached for his gun. The women and children were sent to stay in the largest house in the village.

Later, when Captain Marks looked over the house, he said that it could not be defended against the enemy. He thought it would be safer for the women and children to go to a secret place that he knew far in the deep woods. A man could not be spared to go with them, but Meriwether knew the place and could take the party there.

The boy did not like to leave the settlement when so much was happening, but he obeyed orders. He led the women and children up the bed of a small creek. The water washed away their footprints. They walked a long, long way.

Everyone was glad when they came out in an open space on the bank of the creek. Because they were tired and hungry, a small fire was built. The women cooked food. The children ate and then sat staring quietly into the shadows. Dark night came to the pine woods. Suddenly a noise was heard far off in the forest.

"Indians! Indians!" whispered the little children as they clung to their mothers.

"They'll see us in the firelight!" exclaimed a badly frightened woman.

"What can we do? We'll all be killed!" cried another, equally afraid.

"I'm sure we shouldn't have left the settlement!" said Mrs. Marks.

Meriwether said nothing. He reached over and seized the kettle of water. He threw the water over the fire. Another kettle of water from the creek made the flames die down. The last spark went out. There was deep darkness all around their small camp.

The children stopped crying and the women stopped talking. Everyone sat waiting and listening for something to happen. Then, out of the forest came another sound. It was that of light footsteps made by many moccasined feet. Through the forest only a few yards away passed a long line of figures.

On and on they went into the night. Mothers held their children closer. Even the babies did not whimper. Then there were no more footsteps. There was not a sound. All were gone.

There was no sleep that night, except for the children. Meriwether and the women sat all night long with wide-open eyes. They were near an Indian trail. At any time a passing Indian might attack them.

How glad they were to see the rising sun!

Men from the settlement came in the early morning to see how things were with the party. They brought good news. The Indians had not attacked the settlement. Not one had been seen. No one knew where they had gone.

"They came this way," said Mrs. Marks.

"Here!" exclaimed the men.

"Yes, here. We were warned by a noise far away. Meriwether put out our fire. Then right over there the Indians passed in the darkness."

The men went to look. Down near the creek were many footprints where the Cherokees had crossed. The men looked at one another.

"Our families would have been safer in the settlement," said Uncle Thomas Gilmer. "Anything could have happened to them out here in the woods."

"We'll never send them away again," said Uncle Frank Meriwether. "It is safer for us all to stay together."

136

After a time the Indian scare died away. Neither Cherokees nor Creeks were seen any more in the neighborhood. The men and boys went hunting again.

One day Meriwether and Peachy Gilmer were hunting far from home. They had not seen a single animal. The boys did not want to go home with empty hands. They went on and on.

After a while they crossed a narrow path. They stopped to look.

"This is a game trail," said Peachy. "Let's follow it. Perhaps we'll find a deer."

They went down the trail into the woods. Suddenly they stopped short. There was something hanging beside the trail!

"It's an Indian! Upside down! He must be dead!" exclaimed Peachy. "Let's get out of here fast, Merne!"

The Indian was very much alive, though. He began to kick and swing about.

"Wait!" said Meriwether. "He's caught in a deer noose."

The two boys went nearer. The Indian had stepped into a trap meant for deer and been caught by both feet and jerked off the ground. Other Indians had probably made the trap. To make one, they took a cord of leather and fastened it to the top of a springy tree. Several of them pulled hard on the cord, and bent the tree down. Then they fastened the leather cord to a stick wedged in the trail like a trigger and spread a loop of the cord around it. Then they covered the stick and the loop over thickly with leaves so they didn't show.

If a deer—or a person—stepped on the stick it came loose. Then the bent tree sprang back, jerking the loop tight and lifting whatever was in it. The poor Indian had been so shaken up that he had not been able to reach the cord with his hands, climb up, and loosen the noose.

He expected the boys to kill him. He was ashamed of having been so careless. He glared at them with angry eyes as he swung back and forth. A long red scar made by wildcat claws marked his face.

"Better come away quickly," warned Peachy. "Some other Indians may come along while we're here. I expect to feel an arrow in my shoulders any minute now!"

Meriwether shook his head. "Wait!" he said again. Then he took out his hunting knife and walked toward the Indian. With a quick movement he cut the thong that held the man up. Down came the Indian to the ground. The two boys hurried away. When they turned to look back, the Cherokee was sitting up staring after them. He had a very surprised look on his face.

Since game was so scarce that often the settlement was without meat for days at a time, Meriwether hunted farther and farther away from home. One day he caught sight of a fine fat deer. It was some distance away. He followed it for a long time. At last it went into a big swamp.

Now, none of the men liked to hunt in the swamp. It was a place anything could happen and many things did. There were a few hard paths that were safe to walk on, but most of the swamp was thick black mud that seemed to have no bottom. Animals and men would often sink from sight if they happened to leave the paths.

Meriwether had made up his mind to have the deer. He went right into the swamp after it. The deer ran along a path that wound in and out among the trees. The young hunter followed right after it. Suddenly he felt himself sinking. In trying to keep the deer in sight, he had stepped off the safe path.

The thick soft mud was pulling him down. Meriwether could feel himself going deeper and deeper. The mud was soon up to his knees. The more he struggled the deeper he went. He opened his mouth and called loudly for help—not that he expected anyone to be near, but he could do nothing more for himself.

In answer to his shout an Indian came around a bush. It was the scar-faced Indian of the trail! He had a tomahawk in his hand. When he saw who it was he put the tomahawk aside. Another brave followed.

Both of them took hold of Meriwether. They tugged and pulled and tugged. Suddenly the mud let go with a loud smack and Meriwether found himself standing on the path. Then the two hurried him along the path between them.

"What now?" thought the boy. "Am I a prisoner of the Cherokees?"

Round and round the winding, twisting path they went until at last they stepped out of the swamp onto the solid ground of the green forest.

The scar-faced Cherokee pushed Meriwether

over to a big log and motioned him to stay there. The two Indians went back into the swamp.

In a short time they returned with a deer. Meriwether went to wash some of the mud off his clothes. When he got back venison was broiling over a small fire.

The three ate in silence. When they had fin-

ished, the Indians put the fire out. They were soon ready to go.

"Come," said the scar-faced Indian. They went back into the swamp. In and out they went among the trees and shrubs. The Indians looked here and there, and at last they sighted a fine, fat deer. Then the chase was on. In and out they went. Meriwether always kept the scar-faced Indian in sight, and put his feet carefully in the same places where the Indian had put his.

At last the Indians brought down the deer and one of them carried it on his shoulders until they reached the edge of the swamp. Here he handed it to the surprised boy and started to move away.

"Wait!" said Meriwether, who had been doing some quick thinking.

From his belt he took his father's long hunting knife. It was not easy to give it away, but surely his life was worth a good hunting knife!

"For you," he said, putting it in the scar-faced Indian's hand. Meriwether felt no doubt of the man's pleasure. A smile came to the Indian's lips as he touched the sharp edge with the tip of his finger. He was still smiling when he and his companion silently slipped away among the trees and out of sight.

Return to Virginia

THE years in Georgia were happy ones. The Marks plantation had good crops. More land was cleared of trees.

Captain Marks ran the plantation and gave orders to the servants. Mrs. Marks took care of the house. She found time also to teach the two older boys. There was a little schoolhouse in the settlement, but it was not often that a teacher could be found.

There was really nothing for Meriwether to do at the plantation when school was over. So he went exploring far and wide through the Georgia forests.

The Cherokees and Creeks had left their villages and moved farther away. They no longer came near the settlement. The settlers could live safely in their homes. The danger was past.

The Georgia woods were full of rare plants, trees, and flowers. Meriwether tried to see how many different kinds he could find. He made long lists of what he found. He watched for birds. In winter the woods were full of strange birds from the north. They had come south to get away from ice and snow.

It was fun to collect things. All the boys did it. Each boy collected something different, but Meriwether seemed to be collecting everything.

Chloe did not like the way his room looked. There was too much in it. There were birds' nests, stones, pressed flowers and leaves, and even a dried rattlesnake skin. Chloe hated the snake skin. She wouldn't even touch the seven rattles that hung near the door. In spite of that,

146

Chloe was sorry when the time came for Mister Merne to go back to Virginia.

When Meriwether left, Mrs. Marks said, "Locust Hill is a long way from here. It may be years before I see you again. Study hard at school and learn all you can. In a few years you must take over your plantation. To run it well you must know many things. Let me know what you are doing and what lessons you are having. Be careful on the way. I am glad Jane can come back to Locust Hill to keep house for you."

Meriwether, taking Cuffy along with him, rode away from the Marks plantation. Mrs. Marks did not weep, but there were tears standing in her eyes. Little John Marks cried. Reuben wanted to go with his brother, and he was very angry when he had to stay behind.

"In three years you may go, Reuben," promised his mother.

Old Ruff was not with them today. Only a

week earlier he had followed when Meriwether went hunting.

Ruff knew that his master would send him home. Hunting was too hard for an old dog. So he walked along behind the bushes until they were a mile from home.

Meriwether patted Ruff's head when he came up panting. "Well, old fellow, do you want to go hunting once more?" he asked.

Ruff wagged his tail very fast. Meriwether decided to forget about hunting and just spend the afternoon in the forest with his dog.

The two walked along by the river. When Ruff was tired, his master sat down under a tree. The music of the rippling water soon put both of them to sleep.

While they slept, a dark shadow came stealing silently along the path. It was a hungry wildcat. It smelled the rabbit in Meriwether's hunting bag and wanted it.

Ruff opened one eye. What enemy was this, creeping up to attack his master?

With a loud bark he jumped at the snarling wildcat. Meriwether heard the noise and leaped to his feet. He could not shoot because the two were fighting fiercely.

The wildcat fastened his sharp teeth in Ruff's neck, shook the old dog, and left him lying on the ground. As it turned to run, Meriwether fired and the animal fell.

The old dog was badly hurt. Meriwether carried him home, but in spite of every care Ruff did not get well. His hunting days were over.

The boy was thinking of Ruff as he rode away toward Virginia.

It was Cuffy who first heard the sound of horses' hoofs and said, "Someone's coming, Mister Merne."

The road was lonely. There were no other travelers passing by.

Two rough-looking men rode up beside them. "Good evening, young man," said one as he looked first at Star and then at the good horse which Cuffy was leading. "It's getting late. It's bad to be on the road at this hour. There's a small tavern near here. You would do well to stop there for the night. Come along with us."

Meriwether thought, "They're after the horses, but I can't fight the two of them. Perhaps at the tavern there will be a way." So he rode along with them.

In the tavern yard he saw a little black boy crying. The child was trying to carry two heavy pails of water. Meriwether spoke to Cuffy, who took the pails of water to the kitchen while the child ran along beside him.

The innkeeper and the two men watched Meriwether. When he went inside, they kept between him and the door.

After supper Meriwether went to his room.

150

He shut and locked the door. He had hoped to leave by the window, but the only window was over the room in which the men were sitting.

While he was wondering how to save the horses, a sharp whisper came from a big knot-hole in the wall: "Mister! Come here!"

It was the little black boy.

Meriwether went over.

"Mister," whispered the boy, "bad men downstairs will take your horses. You better go away now. No one's in the stable."

"If I go out this window they'll see me," said Meriwether.

"Come in here. I'll show you how."

Meriwether unlocked his door and slipped out. Then he locked it again and hid the key. He went into the next room. The little boy had the window open.

"Climb down the tree, Mister! Hurry!"

A storm had blown up. The rain fell and

thunder rolled. Meriwether slid down the tree. The boy came after him. Cuffy was in the stable. He had the horses ready.

They led them out through a side door and up over the grassy slope until they were out of sight of the tavern.

"What can I give you?" whispered Meriwether to the boy.

"Nothing, Mister! They see everything. I'd be whipped for helping you. Now go down this path and ride—ride!"

Meriwether pushed a large piece of candy into the child's hand. The boy turned and ran. From between the trees they saw him climbing up the big tree and through the window.

Meriwether rode Star and led the extra horse. Cuffy followed close behind. Out on the dirt road they hurried along. The heavy rain washed out the hoofmarks.

They rode all night and, when morning came,

stopped in deep woods for some much-needed rest. When they awoke, it was afternoon. The horses were still there.

Out on the road they met a planter riding toward home. He invited Meriwether to spend the night at his house.

The next day Meriwether and Cuffy looked at every stranger who came along. The robbers had lost the trail—they were not seen again.

It was a happy day when the travelers finally reached Locust Hill.

Meriwether was glad to find Jane and her family living in the Big House.

The servants had wide smiles. It was good to have Mister Merne home again.

Uncle Nicholas came by to see his favorite nephew. They talked over the important question of where he was to go to school. There was a school for older boys kept by the Reverend Matthew Maury. He lived some twenty miles away. Uncle Nicholas thought it would be a good place for Meriwether to go.

Now, twenty miles was much too far to ride back and forth to school every day. Meriwether had to stay at the Maury home.

He was a good student and studied hard. When weekends came, he was free to go home or to visit some of his many relatives. On these weekend visits many exciting things happened.

One time he was visiting his uncle and aunt at Cloverfields. His little cousin Mildred, who was four years old, was so glad to see him that she followed him wherever he went.

Saturday morning came and Meriwether went hunting. Mildred waved and watched him out of sight. She would have liked to go along.

After the long hours in school, Meriwether enjoyed the day in the woods so much that he stayed until late afternoon.

When Mildred saw him coming, she ran

across the meadow to meet him, her red cape
flying in the breeze.

In the meadow a big bull was chained to a
stake. It was an expensive prize animal—and
it had a very bad temper.

When the bull saw the little girl's red cape,
he was angry. Snorting, he jerked his head about
and pulled until he broke the strong chain that

held him. Then with a wild bellow he started across the field after her.

Mildred heard him and looked back. The fierce animal stopped to paw the earth. He bellowed with anger. Then he came on again. Crying with fear, the little girl ran toward Meriwether. She knew that he would help her.

"Merne!" she cried. "Don't let him get me!"

Meriwether thought fast. He knew what a valuable animal the bull was. His uncle would certainly not want to lose it—but he certainly wouldn't want to lose his little daughter either! There was only one thing to do. He himself could have run fast enough to reach a tree and climb out of danger, but Mildred was too little and too frightened. She would never make it.

"Get behind me, Mildred," he called as he raised his gun. This was one time when he must not miss. If he did they would both be trampled to death by the mad animal.

Mildred scurried by. The tears were running down her cheeks. Meriwether took careful aim and pulled the trigger. The bullet struck the big animal. The bull stopped and shook his head. Then he fell to the ground—dead.

Later on, Meriwether tried to explain the incident to his uncle, who was holding Mildred tightly in his arms.

"Don't say a word, my boy!" his uncle replied. "You did just the right thing. I can always buy another bull, but nothing could ever replace my little girl."

Another time, little Peter McGehee was at Locust Hill. He had come calling with his mother. Peter was eight years old.

He had hoped to go walking in the woods while his mother talked to Cousin Jane. He liked to hear the dry leaves rustle under his feet.

Now Peter sat on the steps with his head on his hands. His mother had said, "No, Peter, you can't go today. Little boys get hurt when they go out alone."

For him the sun was not shining. The world was a dull place. How could he ever be a mighty hunter like Meriwether, if he could not even go alone into the woods?

The young boy jumped when a voice beside him said, "Hello, Peter! Would you like to go squirrel hunting with me? Jane is planning on having squirrel pie for dinner tomorrow."

Peter jumped up. It was Meriwether, tall and strong, who stood there. Then he sat down again and said sadly, "Mother won't let me."

"I'll ask her," said Meriwether, and was gone. He came back with Mrs. McGehee.

"I know how much Peter would like to go with you, Meriwether," she said. "He would like nothing better. Still, we are only calling and we must be driving on soon. You would not be back in time."

"Why not let him stay overnight? I'll bring him home tomorrow."

"That's kind of you, Meriwether. Very well, then, Peter. Stay and go hunting," said Mrs. McGehee with a smile.

Peter smiled back at his mother and went off with his tall friend. All the way across the field he could hardly believe his good luck. He was going hunting at last—and with the best hunter in Albemarle County!

Little Peter never forgot that fine afternoon. The dry November leaves crackled underfoot. An owl blinked from his home in a hollow tree. A crow cawed in the treetop.

They went hunting across the fields and through the mountain lands. At last they came out into a level woodland. A squirrel ran up a locust tree.

Peter held his breath and waited when his friend shot. The squirrel fell. Peter ran to see where the shot went. It had hit the squirrel and gone into the tree.

They saw more squirrels. Meriwether loaded his gun again. With each shot a squirrel fell. Soon they had enough for squirrel pie.

"Now, Peter, how would you like to shoot? Take my gun like this. Hold it level. Now see if you can hit that big tree."

How proud Peter was! He held the rifle just as he was told. He shot three times. Twice he hit the tree. It was a heavy rifle for a small boy.

"You have a good eye, Peter. That's enough for now. When you get your own rifle, shoot at a target until you can always hit the center. Then you will be a good hunter."

New Faces

MERIWETHER was busy trying to grow better crops. Now that he was eighteen years old, it was time for him to take full charge of Locust Hill. His uncles helped him with advice and Meriwether learned quickly.

He was up early in the morning to see that the servants were started at their work. He rode from one field to another to see what could be done. The field servants sang at their work. Everything was right where Mister Merne was.

The years had brought many changes to the family at Locust Hill. Now another great change was to come.

News arrived from Georgia, very sad news. A letter from Mrs. Marks said that Captain Marks had died after a short illness. Meriwether and his brother Reuben were both very sorry. Captain Marks had always been a good friend to the boys. They knew that their mother would miss him sorely.

Mrs. Marks was left alone on the Georgia plantation with the servants and the two small children, John and Mary Marks. She did not wish to stay there. Since Jane, Meriwether, and Reuben were in Virginia, she wished to sell the plantation and come back to Locust Hill.

Meriwether went to talk the matter over with his good friend Mr. Jefferson. Meriwether wanted to know the best way to bring his mother and the two small children back to Virginia.

Mr. Jefferson liked to make plans. He thought for a time. Then he drew a plan for a fine new carriage. The best workmen at Monticello were chosen to work on it. The blacksmiths made a strong iron frame and large wheels with iron rims. The carpenters made the beautiful body of the coach. There were glass windows in each of the heavy doors.

The carriage was to be big and strong. It must be large enough to carry several people. It would be a closed carriage with a high seat in front for the driver. Inside were to be two seats facing each other. There would be room in the back for boxes and trunks, too.

It was many weeks before the coach was finished. One day Mr. Jefferson sent word that the coach was ready. Meriwether hurried over to Monticello to look at it.

It was grand. The outside had a high polish and the seats inside were very soft. Everyone was happy. Mr. Jefferson was pleased because his plan had turned out so well. The workmen were happy over a good piece of work. Meriwether was happy to have such a fine carriage. His mother would enjoy riding in it.

Cuffy and his master set out on the long journey. The roads were poor and the coach was heavy. Four horses were needed to pull the coach over the rough roads. The long, hard journey took several weeks.

Cuffy was a good driver, but even good drivers get into trouble. One day after a heavy rain, the coach stuck in a mudhole. It took a long time to get it free. Another time a broken axle kept them from going on, but at last they reached the Broad River plantation.

Mrs. Marks was waiting for them. She was surprised to see the fine carriage, and she was delighted to see her tall, strong son again. John and Mary climbed in and out of the coach. They wanted to start on the journey at once.

There was much to be done, however, before Mrs. Marks could leave.

164

Meriwether did what he could to help. Finally, one morning, the last package was put into the coach. Relatives and friends gathered around to see them off. Cuffy cracked the whip. The horses pulled. The wheels rolled northward. John and Mary waved to their friends. They were off on the long journey.

The trip back home did not take quite so long. This time there was no broken axle to delay them, and the family had a comfortable ride.

Mrs. Marks was very glad to come again to her lovely old home at Locust Hill. John and Mary were shy at first with big sister Jane and her family, but all the children soon played together. They ran to all corners of the plantation and were often found at Meriwether's side as he walked or rode over the wide fields.

Sometimes he rode with Mary sitting on the saddle before him. John would sit behind and hold onto his big brother's coat.

Now that Mrs. Marks was there to keep house, sister Jane and her family went back to live in Louisa County. The family at Locust Hill was not long alone, though. Three little Marks cousins had been left alone in the world, without a home. Mrs. Marks brought them to Locust Hill to live with her children.

There were lively times at the Big House these days. Whenever Meriwether sat down, the children climbed on his knees and over his broad shoulders.

"Merne," said his mother one day when he came in with the little ones at his heels, "I have never seen anything like it. You might be a fairy piper for the way they follow you about."

The children were not to have Meriwether with them much longer, though. He made a trip out to Kentucky and the Ohio country to see about some land which had been left to little Mary and John Marks. This land had been promised to Captain Marks as pay for being a soldier in the Revolutionary War.

When Meriwether returned, he went to tell Mr. Jefferson about his trip. Now that he had been beyond the mountains, he wanted to go on and see what was in the West beyond the great Mississippi River.

Mr. Jefferson shook his head. "Not yet, my boy. The land out there does not belong to us. Between the Indians and the fur traders you would have a hard time. It would not be safe for you to go alone. They don't want any more white men in the country. Perhaps someday we may send a party of men. Then you shall go."

Soon after this talk, a rebellion broke out among some people in the mountains of Pennsylvania. They did not wish to pay a tax on the goods they made. Young men were asked to go into an army to put down this rebellion. Meriwether said that he would go.

Later he was sent out to the army in Ohio. There had been trouble with the Indians. Meriwether made a good soldier. He liked the army life. He liked his brave general, "Mad" Anthony Wayne. He was moved south and, while stationed near Memphis, he learned the language of the Chickasaw Indians. Later he was sent to the outpost at Detroit. Then Meriwether was promoted. He became Captain Lewis.

One day when he was in camp in Ohio he met an old friend. A tall man came up to him and said, "Sir, aren't you Meriwether Lewis from Albemarle?"

Meriwether looked at the happy face and bright red hair. "Will Clark!" he exclaimed. "What luck to meet you here!"

After this they talked of many things. Meriwether was happy to find that Will was to be his superior officer in the campaign. Will told of his years in Kentucky. Meriwether told of

169

what had happened in Georgia. They both spoke of friends in Virginia and then of Mr. Jefferson whom they liked so much.

"Do you think he will be the next President?" asked Will Clark.

"He's a wise man and would make a good President," answered his friend.

Mr. Jefferson *was* the next President. After he went to Washington, D. C., to live in the White House, he sent a letter to Meriwether. In this letter he asked him to come to Washington and be his secretary. Meriwether would live in the White House and write letters for the President.

Meriwether decided to leave the army and go to Washington. On his way he stopped in Virginia to visit his family. His mother was pleased that Mr. Jefferson had asked him to be his secretary. Of course he must accept. Before he left, though, she needed his help at Locust Hill, to plan the farm work with her and decide what crops should be planted.

They talked of the children. John Marks was a very bright boy. Meriwether wanted his brother to have a good education. Later on John must go to William and Mary College in Williamsburg. Meriwether offered to give him money if he did not have enough to pay his expenses while there.

Secretary to
the President

THE young secretary lived at the White House for almost two years. He liked his work, although he did not like to spend so much time indoors. He liked to meet the famous people who came from all over the world to see President Jefferson.

Mr. Jefferson was a very busy man. He worked long hours to make the United States a good country in which to live.

Meriwether was kept busy too. There were many letters to write and important papers to copy. Sometimes he took notes when Mr. Jefferson talked with statesmen.

The tall, quiet young man had many friends. People invited him to dinners and parties, but he could not always leave the White House.

For exercise Meriwether would rise early in the morning and ride horseback in and around Washington. Sometimes he rode his own horse. If the President could not take his horse out, Meriwether would do it for him. The horse must have exercise.

The idea of making a trip to the Pacific Ocean was still only a dream. Neither the President nor his secretary had forgotten it, though.

One day good news came to the President. France had agreed to sell to the United States the land west of the Mississippi River all the way to the Rocky Mountains.

At once the President began to plan for a group of men to start on a trip across this new country. They would go on to the Pacific Ocean.

The President and Meriwether had often

173

talked over these plans. Meriwether knew that his greatest wish was to come true at last. He was to see what lay beyond the great Mississippi. He was to lead the band of explorers into the unknown land. He would see the wonders that lay beyond the mountains of the West.

The men could not start at once. There were many things that had to be done first.

Meriwether went to Philadelphia to study for several months. He wanted to be able to describe correctly the plants and minerals he might find and to call them by their right names. He had to learn how to use the instruments that would determine locations, just how far west and north the explorers might have gone. He must find out how to make maps.

When this studying was done, Meriwether returned to Washington. After a long talk with the President he started out to buy gifts for the Indians they would meet.

174

It was the President's desire that they make friends with the Indians. Meriwether was to tell them that the White Father in Washington did not wish them to fight.

All the Indian gifts had to be packed. Boats had to be built. The right men must be found to go on the long journey. Special guns were made at Harper's Ferry on the Potomac River, where there was an arsenal.

One day Mr. Jefferson said, "Meriwether, you must choose a man to be second in command on this trip. If you should get sick he could take charge. Who will it be?"

"I know just the man!" exclaimed Meriwether. "Will Clark of Mulberry Hill in Kentucky. We were in the army together. He would make a good leader. Men like him. I wouldn't want him to be second in command, though. It would be better for him to be equal with me."

"You may make him equal if you wish," said

President Jefferson, "but you are in charge. That I will not change."

Will Clark was glad when a letter came from Meriwether. The letter invited him to go on the long journey. He was tired of staying at home and wished to be off at once.

Still, it was many months before everything was ready. Trips were made here and there to get food. Then the food had to be packed in boxes and bundles and tied.

It was on July 5, 1803, that Meriwether Lewis left the White House to meet Will Clark at Louisville. Later in the autumn the two leaders and their forty men reached St. Louis.

It was too late to start up the Missouri River that year, so they made a camp and spent the winter at the mouth of Wood River. They trained their men for life in the wilderness.

Meriwether had another friend with him, a large black Newfoundland dog, which had been offered to him for sale in a river town. Meriwether thought he looked like Ruff, the faithful dog of his childhood. He could do many tricks.

Many times on the long journey the alert black dog saved the party from surprise attacks. His keen nose knew when Indians or wild animals were near. He always slept near his master's tent. Now and then during the night he would awake and ramble about the camp to see if everything was all right.

He went all the way to the Pacific Coast and back with his master.

Exploring New Territory

MERIWETHER had said that William Clark should be a leader of the party with him, and so he was. As things worked out, however, Meriwether was the real chief, who had to make all the hard decisions.

The two finally set out with their company of forty men one fine spring day.

They went up the muddy Missouri River in boats with flat bottoms which had to be rowed along against the current. This was very hard work. It took a long time, weeks and months. Indians looked down at them from the high banks. The Indians came to trade when the explorers stopped for a rest. They were not always friendly. At night the expedition had to camp on islands in the river to be safe from savage attacks.

One night Meriwether awoke to find the sandy ground of the island shaking under him. He jumped up and ordered the men to get into the boats at once. By the time they were safe in the boats the entire island was swept away downstream by the whirling waters. They did not try to land again that night.

Farther up the river was the village of the tall Mandan Indians. The warriors guarded the Missouri. No white men could pass.

Big White, the chief of the Mandans, talked to the white men. He liked the gifts that President Jefferson had sent. They were an officer's coat with gold braid on it, a hat with a long feather, a United States flag, and a medal.

Big White put on his hat and coat. He was

very proud. The other chiefs also received presents, but Big White's were the best.

The chief invited the white men to stay with them for the winter. Meriwether said they would be glad to do so.

Winter came on with ice and snow. Thick ice formed on the river. No boats could get through. The men spent the winter months in a fort which they built near the Mandan village.

The days were very long. Sometimes the men went hunting. When the weather was too bad, they stayed in the fort. One man could play a fiddle and the others would dance jigs to pass the time. The Indians would crowd around to listen to the fiddle and see the white men dance.

Will Clark had brought with him a big, good-natured servant named York. The black man was a surprise to the Indians, for they had never seen one before. The Indians called him the "White-Man-Who-Is-Black," and often gathered around to see York laugh and show his strong, white teeth.

It was at this village that the explorers met Sacagawea, a fine young Indian woman. She was the wife of a trader who lived in the Mandan village. She pronounced her name like this— Săk à ga wē' à. It meant "Bird Girl." It was hard to say and remember, so Will Clark called her "Janey" for short.

When spring came, the Lewis and Clark party left the Mandans and again set out up the muddy Missouri with only thirty men. The others had been sent back to St. Louis with the larger boats. From now on only the smaller boats and canoes would be used.

Letters were sent to President Jefferson telling him how the party had been spending the winter. The boats also carried many gifts to him from the Mandan Indians.

Sacagawea went with them as a guide, carry-

ing her little papoose Pomp on her back. Pomp was a very quiet baby. He looked out at the world with big eyes and did not cry as they went along. When they stopped to rest, his mother would take the cradle off her back and hang it on the branch of a tree. If there was a wind, he swung back and forth. If there was no wind, it was surprising how many of the men found it necessary to pass that way and give the cradle a gentle push. Pomp was indeed a favorite with all.

Sacagawea's husband, who was half French and half Indian, went along as an interpreter. The Indian woman was anxious to get back to her own people. Years before, she had been stolen by another tribe from the Shoshoni Indians who lived far away among the Rockies. Her knowledge of the country and of the Indians was a wonderful help to Meriwether Lewis and Will Clark. She also had such a fine, happy spirit that they grew very fond of her.

Sacagawea proved to be a true heroine. One day a boat overturned in some foaming rapids. In it were important records, instruments, and diaries. Everything went to the bottom of the wild river. Sacagawea quickly laid little Pomp on the bank and dived in after them. Everything was saved. After that the men thought more highly of her than ever.

For days and weeks the men tried to row the canoes and boats up the river. They went only a few miles each day. Many times they would tie towlines to the boats. Then they walked on the shore and pulled the boats along. Some were filled with goods for the Indians. Others held food and supplies for the party. They were so heavily loaded that they were low in the water.

At some time each day the men stopped for a rest. Then two or more hunters would go ashore to look for buffalo or deer. Game was not always found near the river. Meriwether would sometimes travel many miles to bring back a deer. Thirty people needed a great deal of meat to eat. York cooked it for them over the hot coals of the campfire.

The Missouri River grew smaller and more shallow. One day the boats scraped the bottom.

"Take everything out of the boats," said Meriwether. "Hide the boats here in the willows. We'll need them on the way back—if we come this way. Each man must carry a pack until we can buy horses."

There were mountains to be crossed and many long days of travel and suffering from hunger. The men became very thin and tired.

High in the mountains they finally met a tribe of Shoshoni Indians. These were Sacagawea's people and they were friendly.

The Shoshonis had many horses. Sacagawea's brother was chief of the tribe. He was very glad to see his sister again. She told him of the kindness of the white leaders. The Shoshoni Indians had very little food, but they shared what they did have with their guests. The chief wanted them to stay longer. Other tribes came from far away to see the white men.

One day Sacagawea told her brother that the white men had had a good rest and now they must go on. She would go with them. The white men gave many thanks and promises of friendship. There were presents, too. The Indians gave their promises of friendship for all time, and then the explorers went on their way.

Their travels led toward the mighty Pacific Ocean. After many days they came to a large river, the Snake. Here they left the horses with some friendly Indians who promised to care for them. They paid the Indians with bolts of cloth. From there on the way would be by water again. Clumsy boats were made from tree trunks from which the centers had been burned out. They were not very safe because a heavy wave would roll them over. The party went down the Snake River to the Columbia. When the boats went into the Columbia River, the strong current carried them rapidly along.

It was the rainy season, and a thick fog hung over the river. One day they heard great waves breaking on a shore. Here was the mighty Pacific Ocean at last! Meriwether's great dream had come true. Now he knew what lay beyond the great Rocky Mountains. He had explored a new country. He had traveled over land where no other white man had gone. It was the happiest day of his life.

The men built a fort near the fur-trading post, Astoria, at the mouth of the Columbia River in Oregon and spent the winter there. The mountains were too deep in snow for them to return at that time.

President Jefferson had told Meriwether to

take passage on a ship for the return trip. However, not one ship sailed during the winter.

In the spring the men started back overland. It was another long, hard journey. They were often hungry. The tired men were glad when they came to the place where the Indians had kept the horses for them.

Now that they once more had horses to ride, the party got along better. They came at last to where the canoes were hidden in the willows.

From there on was the easiest part of the journey. The mighty Missouri carried the canoes rapidly downstream.

One day in the distance they saw the round houses of the Mandan Indians. Home seemed very near.

Sacagawea came back with the white men to the Mandan village. There they left her. She had seen her own people and was happy.

Back in Washington, President Jefferson was

waiting. No word had come from Meriwether Lewis for a long time. People had begun to say that he might never return.

One day a messenger brought the President good news. It was a letter from Meriwether. He and his men were back at St. Louis. In a few days he would start for home. He wished to know if his mother was well.

Mr. Jefferson was very happy. His young friend was alive. He had made friends with the Indians. The money spent on the trip had brought wonderful results. Now they would know what was in the new territory. Only one man had died.

Mr. Jefferson smiled. He had known how to choose a good leader.

Both Meriwether and Will Clark had kept diaries on the long expedition. Several other men in the party had done so, too.

Each night Meriwether had written down the

important things of the day. He might tell of a canoe that upset and dumped them into the water. Sometimes he wrote of a new river they crossed or of a high range of mountains. Then again he made note of new plants or flowers or mineral deposits that they found.

He sent these interesting and valuable diaries to President Jefferson.

The United States Congress voted to give land to the men who had gone so far. Each man received a certain number of acres. Meriwether had asked that Will Clark be given as much as was given him, but Congress gave Meriwether one thousand five hundred acres and Will Clark one thousand. Meriwether was made governor of all the Louisiana Territory. Will Clark was made Indian Agent and given the title of Brigadier General.

One day Meriwether and Will Clark were very happy. Sacagawea had sent little Pomp to stay with them in St. Louis. He was to live like the white men and go to school.

Meriwether forgot his cares for a time. He laughed and lifted little Pomp high in the air. Then he had him measured for new clothes.

As governor of the great Louisiana Territory, Meriwether had many problems to settle. There were fur traders who broke laws. There were Indian chiefs who came for help against their enemies. Whatever case came up he tried to give a fair, just solution. He knew conditions in the Louisiana Territory better than anyone else. Meriwether Lewis was a good governor and a fine gentleman.

In 1809, on a trip to Washington on government business, Governor Lewis died, ending an already brilliant career.

The Meriwether Lewis National Monument in Lewis County, near Hohenwald, Tennessee, includes his grave and a museum of relics.